1968

POPE'S *DUNCIAD*

POPE'S *DUNCIAD*

A Study of its Meaning

by

Aubrey L. Williams

Archon Books

1968

First published 1955

Reprinted 1968 with permission of
METHUEN & CO., LTD.
in an unaltered and unabridged edition

Library of Congress Catalog Card Number: 68-11258
Printed in the United States of America

TO BETTE

PREFACE

FEW poems have remained so controversial as the *Dunciad* has for more than two centuries. Conceived and created as it was amidst bitter personal strife, the poem has yet managed to preserve a certain massive grandeur in the face of all the passionate attacks it has inspired since Pope's time. And the very fact that it has so long continued to inspire controversy would seem to suggest that the poem has its own indomitable vitality and that it is in direct contact with enduring human issues. We may at times have lost sight of these issues with which the *Dunciad*, on its profoundest level, is concerned, but I do not believe that we have outgrown them.

It is my own conviction, one which has grown steadily since the beginning of this study, that no adequate understanding of the *Dunciad*'s place in literary history is possible until we know more of the way the poem is sustained and nourished by traditions and attitudes which are rooted deep in the medieval and classical past. As this conviction has grown my estimate of my own efforts in this study has become ever more modest. I hope that I have challenged successfully at least a few of the received opinions of the poem; but if I have not then I hope I will have inspired still better efforts to comprehend the poem.

The four major editions of the *Dunciad*—those of 1728, 1729, 1742, and 1743—reveal a progressive expansion of the poem's meaning and imaginative range. I have attempted to organize this study on the basis of these successive editions, focusing as much as possible on problems peculiar to each edition and attempting to realize at the same time the growth in vision revealed by Pope's additions to his poem. The main effort has been critical and interpretative, although I have attempted at the same time to support my arguments and conclusions with a wide variety of historical materials. Throughout the study I have been greatly aided by Mr James Sutherland's admirable edition of the *Dunciad* (Vol. V of The Twickenham Edition of *The Poems of Alexander Pope*, London, Methuen & Co. Ltd, New

Haven, Yale University Press). I have used two cue titles in my text: *Twick. Ed.* refers to Mr Sutherland's edition, and EC refers to *The Works of Alexander Pope* edited by Whitwell Elwin and W. J. Courthope.

In its original form this study was submitted as a dissertation for the degree of Doctor of Philosophy at Yale University, and from its beginnings until the present I have been more than usually fortunate in the number of friendly yet severe critics who have given me the benefit of their learning and wisdom. It is impossible to mention all who have given me advice and criticism, but I particularly wish to thank Mr Martin M. Price, Mr Douglas M. Knight, Mr Stuart G. P. Small, Mr John C. Pope, and Mr Frederick A. Pottle. Mr Hugh Kenner, at one time a fellow student of mine in the Yale Graduate School, contributed in an important way to my own thought on Pope's work. I have a special debt to Mr Marshall McLuhan, whose unpublished Cambridge University thesis, 'The Place of Thomas Nashe in the Learning of His Time', gave me a perspective on Pope's work which I otherwise would not have had. A former student of mine, Mr David G. Baillie III, gave generously of his time and talents; his is the map which is used as an illustration in the text. To Mrs M. M. Price and to Mrs A. W. Hoffman I am indebted for help received in the preparation of the typescript and the map.

There remain three final acknowledgements I wish to make: to Mr Cleanth Brooks, for many years of tolerant and kindly assistance to me in ways which would defy specification; to Mr W. K. Wimsatt, Jr, who in his criticism of this work has been unsparing and who in his kindness to me has been unfailing; to Mr Maynard Mack, who directed this study as a dissertation, who suffered none of its weaknesses gladly, and who touched nothing he did not adorn.

My wife steadfastly refused to have anything to do with this book. For this I am grateful, and to her it is dedicated.

A. L. W.

Silliman College.
Yale University.
  25 March 1955

CONTENTS

*A plan of London and Westminster
is printed on pp. 34 and 35*

ix

INTRODUCTION

THE kinds of attack levelled by Pope at his enemies, said Leslie Stephen, 'make one half ashamed of confessing to reading the *Dunciad* with pleasure'.[1] Such a comment, like so many others that have been made about the *Dunciad*, suggests how strongly the poem has impinged upon not only the artistic sensibilities of readers and critics, but upon their moral sensibilities as well. Like few other works in English literature, the poem appears to occupy a controversial area with regard to which both the moralist and the aesthetician have believed themselves privileged to speak. Even so, it is important to note that no one has seriously maintained that the *Dunciad* as a body of meaning is intrinsically immoral, though it is true that Pope's use of scatological materials and his handling of religious themes have impressed some readers as obscene and blasphemous.

Because the *Dunciad* does not itself approve immoral actions or attitudes, no true problem of the relation between art and morality is raised by the usual attack on the poem. The problem which is raised by such attacks would appear more justly to be one of the relationship which exists between a poet and his art. For it is fairly clear, in this respect, that the objections of the moralistic critic to the poem gain what relevance they have possessed principally from historical and biographical information about Pope and his contemporaries. Because of such information the moralist can say, with some degree of truth, that Pope's attacks on the dunces were often unfair and ill-founded, that personal spite was a major element in the choice of his victims, that Pope's own conduct was so reprehensible that it is hypocritical of him to censure others. To state the objections in their baldest terms (as they have often been stated), Pope was a liar and a hypocrite who maligned the characters and literary efforts of others. From this point of view, the *Dunciad* appears to

1. Leslie Stephen, *Alexander Pope*, in the English Men of Letters series, ed. by John Morley (New York, 1880), p. 120.

lose much of its status as a poem; it appears, instead, to be more
of a gigantic libel than anything else.

It is rather obvious that criticism in the past has shown little
tendency to regard the *Dunciad* as in any way separable from the
personality of its author. It has usually tended, on the contrary,
to refer the poem back to Pope's personality, and then to read
the poem as an expression, largely malignant, of that personality. Such an approach generally begins 'by trying to derive the
standard of criticism from the psychological *causes* of the poem
and ends in biography'; the usual result of such an approach is
that 'the poem itself, as an object of specifically critical judgement, tends to disappear'.[1] Critics of the poem who have adopt-
ed such a procedure usually cast their judgements in terms of
Pope's intentions and motives (Pope 'endeavoured to sink into
contempt all the writers by whom he had been attacked, and
some others whom he thought unable to defend themselves'[2]),
or of his feelings ('the feeling displayed surpassed in virulence
and intensity that manifested towards the man[3] who occasioned
the satire itself'[4]), or of his neurological instability ('Pope finds
himself unable to re-settle the equilibrium in his nervous system
until he has taken out his revenge by an extra kicking adminis-
tered to some old mendicant or vagrant lying in a ditch'[5]).

That a criticism which refers most of its findings back to the
person of the poet has been unfair to the *Dunciad* as a poem is at
least an arguable conclusion. But at the same time it should be
admitted that, if ever a poem has conspired, by its very nature,
to tempt a critic into such a procedure, the *Dunciad* is that poem.
Because the poem uses historical circumstances and real personalities as the very stuff of its composition it never appears to

1. W. K. Wimsatt, Jr, and M. C. Beardsley, 'The Affective Fallacy', *The
Sewanee Review*, 57 (1949), p. 31.
   2. Samuel Johnson, 'Pope', *Lives of the English Poets*, ed. Arthur Waugh,
The World's Classics Series (London, Oxford University Press, 1942), II,
p. 275.
   3. Lewis Theobald, king of the dunces in the earlier versions of the
Dunciad.
   4. Thomas Lounsbury, *The Text of Shakespeare* (New York, Charles Scrib-
ner's Sons, 1906), p. xv.
   5. Thomas De Quincey, 'Lord Carlisle on Pope', in *The Collected Writings
of Thomas De Quincey*, ed. David Masson (Edinburgh, 1890), XI, pp. 126–7.

be an entirely fictional creation. The *Dunciad* insists, in fact, that
a reader be aware of its historical connections and its relevance
to real personalities; a good deal of the poem's comic tension
stems from such an awareness, as we shall see later on. The
poem's own demand for such an awareness, therefore, has stimulated the type of investigation which often ends in biography.
A poem cannot require that a critic be aware of so much, and no
more. What is the point beyond which a legitimate historical
awareness passes over into personality study? One may not be
able to establish such a point at all, but one can distinguish between a method of approach which 'involves close historical
study but remains aesthetic criticism' and one which ends up as
'sociology, biography, or other kinds of non-aesthetic history'.[1]

Much of the moralistic tinge which has characterized criticism of the *Dunciad* in the past would appear to be the logical
consequence of an emphasis upon the poet's personality and its
expression in his work. Once the study of a work of art has lost
its dominantly aesthetic orientation the way is cleared for judgements based upon many considerations other than aesthetic
ones. Biography and the study of history quite legitimately inspire a process of moral evaluation. As facts in general human
experience, moreover, both Pope and his artistic activities are
quite subject to a moralistic evaluation. A poet who writes such
a poem as the *Dunciad* may quite possibly deserve the moral dis-
approval of his fellows and may even be subject to action for
libel. I am not so sure that in either event he is proved to have
written a poor poem. Yet moral condemnation of Pope more
than once has influenced critical estimation of his art. There
was Macaulay's essay, whose 'damaging effect on Pope's fame
is mainly due', as Oscar Maurer has said,[2] 'to the highly coloured
and violently unfavourable estimate of Pope as a man', and
there was Elwin's influential criticism, in the great nineteenth-
century edition of the poet's work, which undermined Pope's
standing as a satirist on the grounds that his 'private life gave

1. W. K. Wimsatt, Jr, and M. C. Beardsley, 'The Intentional Fallacy',
The Sewanee Review, 54 (1946), pp. 472–3.
2. 'Pope and the Victorians', *The University of Texas Studies in English*, 24
(1945), p. 212.

him no right to exercise the function of a *censor morum*'.[1] Often the objections of the moralistically inclined critics appear reducible to the problem of whether or not an immoral man (and here we may dismiss for the moment the question of whether or not Pope was more immoral than most of the rest of us) can write a good poem. If the moralist's objections were really reducible to such a simple formulation one might advance enough evidence to show that immoral men frequently do compose excellent works of art.

In any satiric work art stands in close and peculiar relationship with morality from the beginning. Such works appear to spring from a blend of the artistic faculties and of the moral attitudes, either real or assumed, within the satirist. The satirist, either in terms of biographical reality or in terms of a fictive personality, takes a moral position from which he lashes out at what appear to be, in the light of his own or his assumed standards, the vices and follies of mankind.[2] In one way or another the question of morality is raised by the artist himself. It could be wished that his moral position within the framework of his art might be regarded as privileged, or at least that criticism of his moral stance within the poem be unprejudiced by knowledge of his character outside the poem, or that criticism of his own moral position be distinguished from criticism of his art. But human nature does not readily compartmentalize its judgements, and so it is hardly to be wondered at if moral and aesthetic judgements about the *Dunciad* have often been sadly entangled. The situation can become even more vexing if, as in the case of Pope, the satirist assumes a personality within the province of his art which is widely at variance, in the eyes of many of his readers at least, with that which he has in real life.

When such a situation occurs it is all too likely that a critic will say, as has been said about Pope, something like this: 'How can we accept lofty condemnation of the vices and weaknesses of mankind from an author who garbled his own correspondence in order to give a false idea of his relations to great men of letters,

1. Ibid., p. 222.
2. The essay by Maynard Mack, 'The Muse of Satire', in *The Yale Review*, 41 (1951–2), pp. 80–92, is relevant to most of my discussion here.

and descended to the meanest and most tortuous devices to
secure their publication in such a way that he might afterward
denounce it as piratical ?'[1] The view of the relationship between
an artist and his work which is implied by such a question has
little validity, in my opinion, as a literary judgement. But such
views have influenced the estimate of Pope's achievement in the
Dunciad for a long time and are likely to continue to do so. One
may deplore such views, but they appear to be inevitable accre-
tions to a situation which the *Dunciad*, by its emphasis on the
historical relevance of its meaning and by its inaccurate portrayal of historical personalities, has helped to create.

Preoccupied with condemnation of the element of personal
passion that may have inspired Pope's attacks on his enemies
and his falsification of their personalities in the *Dunciad*, the
moralistic critic is often unable to see with Émile Montégut that,
'like the marvelous lance which heals the wounds that it has
made, the passion which injured the composition of the poem
has at the same time doubled and tripled its range', and that by
this same passion the dunces 'are transformed into an immense
race and elevated to the stature of *criminels de lèse-intelligence, de
lèse-moralité, de lèse-civilisation*'.[2]

As Pope's personal enemies enter into his poem they are transformed, but the transformation is possible only by a falsification
of their real personalities. The dunces are *not* altogether the
same as they were in real life; they have been given a symbolic
importance which they lacked in reality. A falsification of personality which, from a strictly moralistic point of view, may be
considered reprehensible, can be seen, from a different point of
view, as the very source of much of the poem's imaginative
power.

Portions of even such poems as *Paradise Lost* and *The Faerie
Queene* should remind us that no great or extensive work of art
comes to us unimpaired by the passage of time. The *Dunciad* has
suffered from the same cause, and no amount of foot-noting can

1. Cited by Maurer, p. 232. See the anonymous review, 'Courthope's Life
of Pope', in *The Church Quarterly Review*, 30 (1890), p. 404.
2. Émile Montégut, 'Heures de Lecture d'un Critique—Pope', *Revue des
Deux Mondes*, 86 (1888), p. 312.

revivify for us every detail of the poem. In addition, as is all too likely in the case of satire, changing moral norms and attitudes toward the nature of mankind have further enfeebled, for many readers since Pope's time, the poem's relevance and authority. To readers of the nineteenth century with a romantic bias in their thinking much of the poem was certain to appear to be perverse or cruel. Similarly perverse or cruel will the poem appear today, perhaps, to a person of strongly secular or humanitarian views. Finally, there has been the effect wrought on the poem's reputation by various and changing aesthetic criteria. The poem was not likely to fare well in a period when Pope and Boileau could be described as the 'greatest disciples of the bad school of stiff, formal, pedantic, sapless classicism',[1] or when a critic could deplore the fact that Pope had 'not the seeing eye and hearing ear of an outdoor man',[2] or complain that Pope 'has written none of the verses which children love, nor any lines which grown-up people care to croon over in moments of weakness or sorrow'.[3]

It is to be hoped that we are still capable of valuing works which are not, from the critical standpoint of any age, artistically impeccable. *The Rape of the Lock* is by far a more perfect poem than the *Dunciad*, but there seems to me to be little doubt that the latter poem has the vaster range and that it is much more profound. One must grant that Pope is at times in the *Dunciad* clumsy in the treatment of his material and that at other times he is over-subtle. One may admit that, with the addition of a fourth book to the original three-book version of the poem, the *Dunciad*'s overall structure ultimately breaks down. In addition, so weighty and, occasionally, so unassimilated are the materials of history and personality that the poem's organizing principles and central themes at times struggle through the mass of detail painfully, if at all. The poem itself must share part of the blame if it has been so often misread or under-read, and it is not re-

1. Charles Mackay, 'Boileau and Pope', *The Nineteenth Century*, 10 (1881), p. 852.
2. Cited by Maurer, p. 231. See the review of the EC edition of Pope's works in *The Edinburgh Review*, 160 (1884), p. 314.
3. Cited by Maurer, p. 214. See John Dennis, *Studies in English Literature* (London, 1876), p. 60.

markable that some critics have called it plainly a bad poem. At the same time, one should give due consideration to the quite high esteem in which the poem has often been held. Johnson described the *Dunciad* as one of Pope's 'greatest and most elaborate performances';[1] Thackeray singled out the poem for very high praise;[2] De Quincey, who as much as anyone in the nineteenth century attacked Pope both as man and poet, asserted that the libels on Pope by the dunces 'drew forth, for the everlasting admiration of posterity, the very greatest of Pope's works—a monument of satirical power the greatest which man has produced, not excepting the "MacFleckno" of Dryden—namely, the immortal "Dunciad".'[3] Ruskin's rather too enthusiastic opinion was that 'the *Dunciad* is the most absolutely chiselled and monumental work "exacted" in our country',[4] and even Leslie Stephen stated that 'the *Dunciad* . . . is in some respects [Pope's] masterpiece'.[5]

One cannot, of course, resolve questions of literary merit by citing authorities. I have cited them only because the rather intemperate views of critics such as Elwin, Lounsbury, and Highet have so often tended to dominate critical thinking about the *Dunciad* and to obscure the real respect the poem has elicited over a long period of time from eminent men of letters. It is only fair to concede the truth of many objections which can be brought against the poem. But it is also only fair to insist that many of the critics who have objected to the *Dunciad* have given little if any evidence in their writings that they had made a serious attempt to understand the poem in its full complexity. This study does not aim to show that the objections of previous critics were all unfounded, but it does aim to show that, by looking at the *Dunciad* in a light somewhat different from that usually employed, one may perceive values and meanings in it which appear to have been generally disregarded in the past. Emphasis

1. *Lives of the English Poets*, II, p. 275.
2. William Makepeace Thackeray, *English Humourists*, intro. by G. A. Watrous (New York, Thomas Y. Crowell & Co., 1902), pp. 115–16.
3. De Quincey, *The Collected Writings*, IV, p. 270.
4. John Ruskin, 'Lectures on Art', in *The Works of John Ruskin*, eds. E. T. Cook and Alexander Wedderburn (London, George Allen, 1905), XX, p. 77.
5. *Alexander Pope*, p. 117.

B

has been placed on the positive qualities of the *Dunciad*, not because I wished to brush aside as of no importance valid objections to the poem, but rather because it seemed unnecessary to rehearse a body of objections which, through repetition, by now have become thoroughly standardized.

It is a simple truth, but one that is often overlooked, that certain poems, and forms of poetry, offer values which are not to be found in any other poems. The *Dunciad* may ultimately be classified as only a 'magnificent failure'. But the English literary tradition does not offer many, if any, great works of complete perfection, and so we can hardly afford to ignore the magnificence, in whatever circumstances and however impaired, which that tradition bequeaths us. The *Dunciad* is not so limited by the personal quarrel which may have inspired it that it does not rise to the contemplation of larger issues which have been, and undoubtedly always will be, the preoccupation of mankind. As Émile Montégut pointed out, 'this work, in spite of its faults, and even because of its faults, reveals strongly the pre-eminent merit of Pope's genius. A satire directed against his contemporaries who are for ever lost in obscurity, it would be absolutely unreadable today, if an idea of general and eternal interest was not its principle and aim. Pope saw in bad taste, dulness, folly, and all the other infirmities of the literary spirit, when they have grown arrogant, the first cause of the perversion of moral ideas, and by consequence, of the decadence of nations'.[1]

1. *Revue des Deux Mondes*, 86 (1888), p. 313.

CHAPTER I

THE DUNCIAD OF 1728

I

THE *Dunciad*, Pope says, was written in the days when 'Paper . . . became so cheap, and printers so numerous, that a deluge of authors cover'd the land'.[1] With a flood of poetic trifles and invectives, party pamphlets, scandalous 'true histories', and vulgar farces pouring daily from the presses, there appeared to be little hope of maintaining the principles and standards of literature, largely derived from the classic past, so revered by the Augustans. It was a time when admired passages of Virgil and Horace were warped into the poetic fabrics of birthday odes and flattering epistles, when an anarchic synthesizer such as 'Orator' Henley considered himself the restorer of the 'lost arts' of rhetoric and elocution,[2] when Ambrose Philips was judged inferior only to Virgil and Theocritus in the writing of pastoral,[3] when it was said of Sir Richard Blackmore that 'he may justly be reckon'd the *Next* to, though not an *Equal* with *Homer* and *Virgil*'.[4] In the literary order it seemed to many Augustans as if chaos were come again, as if modern dwarfs, by sheer weight of numbers, were about to overwhelm the giant figures of Greece and Rome. A host of undistinguished writers, the heirs of the 'swarms of new writers'[5] hatched out in the time

---

1. See 'Martinus Scriblerus, of the Poem', *Twick. Ed.*, p. 49.
2. John Henley, *A Guide to the Oratory* (London, 17[?]), p. 13. See also Henley's *The First Sermon Preach'd at the Opening of the Oratory, On Sunday, July 3. 1726* [London, 1726], p. 38.
3. See Charles Gildon's *The Complete Art of Poetry* (London, 1718), I, p. 157. In *Guardian* no. 32 (Friday, 17 April 1713) Philips was described as the legitimate heir to the great pastoral writers of the past: 'Theocritus . . . left his dominions to Virgil; Virgil left his to his son Spenser; and Spenser was succeeded by his eldest-born, Philips.'
4. This was the opinion of a contemporary translator of René Le Bossu's *Traité du poëme épique*. See *Monsieur Bossu's Treatise of the Epick Poem*, trans. by W. J. (London, 1719), I (a 3)ᵛ.
5. See James Sutherland's *A Preface to Eighteenth Century Poetry* (Oxford, Clarendon Press, 1950), p. 41.

9

of Charles II, appeared to be debasing the classical resources, their strength and sublimity, by applying them to mean ends. Even Pope's victims, though they themselves might be contributing to the deterioration of letters, sometimes shared in the gloom[1] aroused by such a state of affairs and occasionally expressed their apprehensions. Welsted speaks of the present 'conjuncture, in which I know not what black clouds seem to lower over arts and sciences, when men are daily falling from all sense of politeness, and an almost universal depravation of taste is spread through the kingdom'.[2]

The age was a time of great and profound changes, changes which many could only view, though perhaps mistakenly, with deep pessimism. Scientific and philosophical developments of the seventeenth century were effecting radical modifications in the old attitudes and values. At the same time the traditional social and political structures were feeling the strain caused by the growth of a large and powerful middle-class. The tastes of a broad new class of readers, barely literate by Pope's standards, were being satisfied, and pandered to, by writers who appeared to many to be, if not totally ignorant of a great literary tradition, at least irresponsible in their obligations toward that tradition. In addition, there was the effect wrought on the literary scene by the release of a race of hired political writers, some of whom could be persuaded, as Defoe was,[3] to write for both the Whigs and the Tories simultaneously. As Pope points out in one of his notes to the *Dunciad*, it was estimated by a committee appointed to investigate Walpole's administration that 'no less than *fifty-thousand, seventy-seven pounds, eighteen shillings*, were paid to Authors and Printers of News-papers, such as Free-Britons, Daily-Courants, Corn-Cutter's Journals, Gazetteers, and other political papers, between Feb. 10, 1731. and Feb. 10, 1741'.[4]

1. See Louis I. Bredvold's essay, 'The Gloom of the Tory Satirists', in *Pope and His Contemporaries: Essays Presented to George Sherburn*, ed. James L. Clifford and Louis A. Landa (Oxford, Clarendon Press, 1949), pp. 1–19.
2. Leonard Welsted, *Works, in Verse and Prose* (London, 1787), p. 212. The remark is found in Welsted's Dedication to *The Dissembled Wanton*.
3. See Laurence Hanson, *Government and the Press, 1695–1763* (London, Oxford University Press, 1936), pp. 101–5.
4. *Twick. Ed.*, p. 311, note to l. 314. See also Hanson, p. 118: 'So great was the uproar caused by the disclosure of the extent of [Walpole's subsidies

The vision offered in the *Dunciad* of an England on the verge of a cultural breakdown is certainly a historical exaggeration, but it was an exaggeration born of a real sense, shared by many Augustans, of a threat to traditional and highly esteemed values. As R. H. Griffith has pointed out, what Pope and others 'experienced' was a 'wave of wrong methods, wrong standards' which appeared to be 'threatening the extinction of Learning in England'.[1] Doubtless many persons were unduly alarmed by the changes that were taking place about them. There have been bad writers in every age, and traditional values are continually subject to attack and modification. In addition, many in the age were unable to see very much of the good which was obtained only by a sacrifice of the old ways of thinking and doing. But though the prophets of cultural doom were proved to be at least partly wrong by future events, and though a decided bias is to be found in their estimate of the contemporary scene, we must still approach the *Dunciad* with some sense of the urgency with which many Augustans viewed what they considered to be a historical crisis. The question of whether or not England actually stood on the brink of cultural disaster is not so important for our purposes as the fact that Pope and many of his contemporaries thought that it did.

The threat to time-honoured values was most clearly mirrored for many Augustans in the contemporary assault on classical standards and traditions in literature. The classical models and resources appeared to be perverted and debased by a variety of abuses—inappropriate borrowings and applications, mean imitations, vulgar paraphrases. At the same time, however, the classical resources remained, in their original splendour, a perpetual reproach to those in the present who were guilty of such abuse. The very introduction of classical materials into the work of a bad writer automatically supplied a standard by which such work could be measured and found wanting. A Blackmore might write epics in which he imitated

to the press] that no ministry in the immediate future could dare to pursue like measures.'

1. See Griffith's review of James Sutherland's edition of the *Dunciad* in *PQ*, 24 (1945), p. 156.

celebrated portions of the *Aeneid*, but the base metal of the imitations would only reflect the more dully in the light of their
source. Whatever the distortion or adulteration of the classical
resources, the Augustan age was a period in which the literary
pretensions and attainments of even the least accomplished
writer inevitably called for evaluation in the light of classical
models.

The outcome of this inevitable evaluation was the now little
understood 'War of the Dunces', a controversy compared to
which the previous conflict between the Ancients and Moderns
appears (not that it was) relatively impersonal and remote from
human passions. By contrast to the long-range hostilities of the
earlier quarrel, the War of the Dunces was marked by the sort
of emotional clamour and personal outrage described by Savage
as occurring when the *Dunciad* first was vended: 'a Crowd of
Authors besieg'd the Shop; Entreaties, Advices, Threats of Law,
and Battery, nay Cries of Treason were all employ'd, to hinder
the coming out of the *Dunciad*: On the other Side, the Booksellers and Hawkers made as great Efforts to procure it'.[1] The
War of the Dunces was, in many respects, closely related to the
Ancients and Moderns controversy;[2] but it was also a civil war
fought out among practising poets and authors, one that arose
from the threat to standards of good writing believed by one
party to be created by the works of the other. That the war
occurred on this level undoubtedly accounts for the amount and
intensity of the personal abuse involved.

The threat contained in the literature of the dunces was not
the frank, openly belligerent assault on the past which such a
'modern' as William Wotton had made; the new attack was
insidious, even unconscious of itself. The highly sophisticated
analogy drawn by Pope in his 'Epistle to Augustus' between
George II and Augustus Caesar is nothing more, in one respect,
than what Eusden and Cibber did innocently and uncritical-
ly in their birthday odes.[3] As the Earl of Shaftesbury summed

1. Richard Savage, *A Collection of Pieces in Verse and Prose, Which have been
publish'd on Occasion of the Dunciad* (London, 1732), p. vi.
2. The relationship is discussed in Chap. v.
3. Maynard Mack has pointed this out in his essay ' "Wit and Poetry and

up the contemporary practice upon which Pope was to refine,

> Our ENCOMIUM or PANEGYRICK is as fulsom and displeas-
> ing; by its prostitute and abandon'd manner of Praise. The
> worthy Persons who are the Subjects of it, may well be
> esteem'd Sufferers by the Manner. And the Publick, whether
> it will or no, is forc'd [by the comparison of the subjects to
> Virgil, Augustus, Tully, and others] to make untoward Re-
> flections, when led to it by such *Satirizing Panegyrists*. For in
> reality the Nerve and Sinew of modern *Panegyrick* lies in a dull
> kind of Satir; which the Author, it's true, intends shou'd turn
> to the advantage of his Subject; but which, if I mistake not,
> will appear to have a very contrary Effect.[1]

The artistic and critical irresponsibility which many in the age
detected was not at all designed to vitiate classical literary
values. But such irresponsibility inevitably caused, in one
Augustan view, a deterioration in taste and, more important,
a correlative deterioration in morals and manners.

The importance, for the Augustan argument as well as for our
own understanding of the *Dunciad*, of the connection between
taste and character, art and morals, cannot be overstressed.
Taste was considered by the Augustans (as by poets and writers
for centuries before them) to be an index to character, a visible
sign of an inner and more fundamental condition. John Brown's
pessimistic evaluation of the nation's character as indicated by
the prevailing taste may be somewhat extreme—he judged England to be 'rolling to the Brink of a Precipice that must destroy'
it[2]—but the following passage of Oldmixon is a typical expression of the relationship thought to exist:

> Good Judges foresaw it twenty or thirty Years ago, and
> mark'd the Gradations by which this Decay wou'd appear
> sensibly. They, probably, made those Reflections from what

Pope'': Some Observations on His Imagery', in *Pope and His Contemporaries*,
ed. James L. Clifford and Louis A. Landa, p. 34.
    1. See Anthony Ashley Cooper, 3rd earl of Shaftesbury, *Characteristicks of
Men, Manners, Opinions, Times*, 2nd edition (London, 1714), I, p. 226.
    2. See *An Estimate of the Manners and Principles of the Times* (London, 1757),
p. 15. See, in addition, Brown's *Essays on the Characteristics* (London, 1755),
where the evaluation of the nation's character in such terms is found throughout.

they had observ'd of the Fate of Poetry and Eloquence; when, after the Age of *Augustus*, *Mimes*, *Cudgel-Players*, and *Bears*, were preferr'd to *true Comedy*; the Points of *Martial* to the happy turns of *Catullus*; when Sound got the better of Sense, and solid Reason gave Way to Tales and Trifles; when the Degeneracy reach'd their Morals as well as their Arts and Sciences, (as it will always do in all Countries) and the Loss of their Taste was follow'd with the Loss of their Liberty.[1]

The condition of the arts, then, was regarded as symptomatic; values in arts presupposed broader and bigger values. The inundation of England by purveyors of bad art, and the untutored or degenerate taste which hailed their literary efforts, was a 'conjuncture' of events suggesting a general slackening in the moral and social fibre of the nation. This perspective on art is that which is important above all else for a study of the *Dunciad*, for the fundamental procedure in that poem is the use of artistic deterioration as the metaphor by which bigger deteriorations are revealed. Pope has converted the general Augustan tendency to view art as symbolic into a highly flexible poetic technique, turning bad writers, bad writing, and bad taste into imagery of moral and social significance. His refinement upon the diagnostic inclinations of his contemporaries can be illustrated by the opening lines of the *Dunciad*:

> Books and the Man I sing, the first who brings
> The Smithfield Muses to the Ear of Kings.
> Say great Patricians! (since your selves inspire
> These wond'rous works; so Jove and Fate require)
> Say from what cause, in vain decry'd and curst,
> Still Dunce the second reigns like Dunce the first?
>
> (I 1–6)[2]

When the king and his nobility began to patronize the farces and pantomimes (compare Oldmixon's mimes and cudgel-players)—which in the past had been the fare of the vulgar and confined to such areas as Smithfield—the event must have im-

1. From John Oldmixon's very free translation of *The Arts of Logick and Rhetorick*, by Father Dominique Bouhours (London, 1728), p. x.
2. All line references to the *Dunciad* in this chapter, unless otherwise noted, are to the A text of the *Twick. Ed.*

pressed many a sensitive mind as a signal indication of a decline in values, an emblem of a general debilitation in the character of the age. And in Pope's poem such events are made to disclose to us a vision of the same sort.

In its subject matter—the corruption of traditional literary standards, the misuse of verbal art—the *Dunciad* is certainly involved with the local, the personal, the contemporary. What we must resist firmly, however, is the tendency to view the poem as if it were mainly of biographical and historical interest, simply the record of a bitter feud between Pope and his enemies. The poem is not so firmly embedded in the matrix of history that we cannot attain the perspective of the Augustans, cannot see the literary perversions of dunces, whether biographical or imaginary, as the correlatives of greater disorders in a wider realm of values. In the *Dunciad* bad art constantly asserts its metaphorical status, and though the vehicle at times may be real live dunces and their actual writings, it is a vehicle which embodies a universal significance.

The last point can be illustrated by one of the most important statements Pope made about his poem. Speaking of its one, great, and remarkable action, he says that it is 'the introduction of the lowest diversions of the rabble in *Smithfield* to be the entertainment of the court and town; or in other words, the Action of the Dunciad is the Removal of the imperial seat of Dulness from the City to the polite world; as that of the Æneid is the Removal of the empire of *Troy* to *Latium*'.[1] This statement progresses from a view of the action as a contemporary actuality—the admission of Smithfield pleasures to the court—to the idea that the art of the duncesis an analogue of a mythical empire, that of Dulness, the deity of Pope's poem. The advance of Dulness's seat of empire from the city to the polite world will constitute, as we shall see later in this chapter, a displacement of higher values by baser values. Such a dislodgement of values, the substitution of the bad for the good, is not a matter of mere historical curiosity: it is a universal and enduring human concern.

1. See 'Martinus Scriblerus, of the Poem', *Twick. Ed.*, pp. 50–1.

II

Though the *Dunciad* is avowedly an imitation of classical epic, complete, Pope asserted, with 'one, great, and remarkable action', yet, from the time of John Dennis to the present day, critics and editors have substantially agreed that a major deficiency of the poem has been its lack of an 'action'. Recent writing on the *Dunciad* supports this criticism: Sutherland agrees with Warton and Dennis that the poem 'lacks action'.[1] Gilbert Highet says the 'poem is, as Croker observes, a series of episodes'.[2] Austin Warren states that Pope's parody 'suffers from having no real plot or fable',[3] and Tillotson says that the *Dunciad*, in contrast to *The Rape of the Lock* (which he calls the 'exquisitely diminished shadow cast by an *entire* epic'), is the 'ludicrous, grotesque, lifesize shadow cast by a *piece* of an epic poem'.[4] Nearly all the complaints express the conviction that the hero of Pope's poem, Lewis Theobald, does nothing. This criticism is summed up by Courthope:

> the action of the 'Æneid' is exhibited in the acts of Æneas the hero; in the 'Dunciad', on the other hand, we are told only of one action of the hero, viz., the preparations to burn his works in the First Book; the Second Book is entirely episodical; in the Third Book the hero merely dreams; and in the Fourth he is asleep . . . Though the parodies in the first three books are admirably contrived for the purpose of bringing particular dunces into contempt, they have little relevancy to the proposed action of the poem.[5]

By overemphasizing the fact (true, in a sense, beyond ques-

1. *Twick. Ed.*, pp. xli–xlii.
2. ' "The Dunciad" ', *M.L.R.*, 36 (1941), p. 336. In his introduction to the *Dunciad* (EC, IV, p. 21) W. J. Courthope states that the poem is a 'series of episodes'. I have been unable to find such a description of the poem by J. W. Croker, who collected a great deal of material towards the Elwin-Courthope edition of Pope's works, but wrote none of the introductory material.
3. *Alexander Pope as Critic and Humanist* (Princeton, Princeton University Press, 1929), p. 172.
4. Geoffrey Tillotson, *On the Poetry of Pope*, 2nd edition (Oxford, Clarendon Press, 1950), p. 55.
5. EC, IV, pp. 21–2.

tion) that the *Dunciad* has no action that we can say is exhibited in the acts of its hero, past critics have failed to see that the poem does have the analogy of an 'action', an analogy which conforms to the way in which Pope's contemporaries defined the action of classical epics, and which is precisely what the *Dunciad* needs to accomplish its main design. Granting at once, then, that the poem does not have the kind of action these critics expected of it (and reserving for the moment the question whether this very fact is not a significant part of the poem's total comment on the age), we may still reasonably suspect, in view of Pope's own explicit statements, that it has an 'action' or 'movement' of a type that we can only disengage by approaching the poem from another direction. No one, for example (so far as I know), has sufficiently weighed the warning from the Publisher (i.e., Pope) to the Reader of the 1728 *Dunciad*: 'by the frequency of his allu-sions to *Virgil*, and a *labor'd* (not to say *affected*) *shortness* in imita-tion of him, I should think him [the author of the *Dunciad*] more an admirer of the *Roman* Poet than of the *Grecian*'.[1] This state-ment is susceptible, perhaps, of two interpretations: it may refer merely to a brevity and concentration of meaning Pope attempted to achieve in his verse; or it may suggest that the *Dunciad* is a laboured and affected, though highly condensed, imitation of the *Aeneid*. In the light of the evidence to be pre-sented in a moment it seems to me that we are warranted in at least considering the second of the alternatives. But in any event the passage definitely emphasizes the connection of Pope's poem with Virgil rather than with any other classical writer. This is important because most critics have seen the *Dunciad* as an attempt to imitate classical epic *in general*, not as a foreshortened imitation of one particular epic, the *Aeneid*. The result of this mistaken opinion has been that the 'action' or 'movement' of Book I of the *Dunciad*, which provides the framework for all that follows in the poem, has remained unrecognized or misunder-stood.

But an even more important pronouncement by Pope is that other already quoted, where the poet informs us that the action of his poem is the removal of the empire of Dulness from the City

1. *Twick. Ed.*, p. 204.

of London to the polite world, Westminster, just as the action of
the 'Æneid is the Removal of the empire of *Troy* to *Latium*'. In
other words, we have the destruction of one empire, in Pope's
poem as in Virgil's, and the establishment of another. What
seems to have been disregarded by past critics is the fact that in
the *Dunciad* the 'City' of London figures metaphorically as
'Troy'—it stands for the imperial seat of Dulness and is at the
same time an imaginary 'Troy', while the court world to the
west becomes the Latium, the 'Rome', to which that seat of
empire is to be transported. Since in 1728 the City was clearly
set off from the polite world in Westminster by the portions of
the old city wall still standing,[1] and since London town was traditionally known as Troy-novant, Pope was able to make this
imaginative relationship with a good deal of aptness and ease.
Unless we grasp this adaptation of the Virgilian myth in the
poem, we are not likely to understand the real function of the
parodies of the *Aeneid*. The fall of the new fictive 'Troy', for instance, is presented as taking place upon the death of Elkanah
Settle, the last of the City Poets and thus a staunch defender of
the City. Pope says in one of his notes: 'This important point of
time [the death of Settle] our Poet has chosen, as the Crisis of the
Kingdom of *Dulness*, who thereupon decrees to remove her
imperial seat from the City, and over-spread the other parts of
the Town'.[2] It is in the light of this same fictive situation, moreover, that we first glimpse Theobald, the duncely 'Aeneas' of
Pope's poem. Here he laments the approaching collapse of this
mythic empire (which he expressly calls 'Troy'), addressing the
goddess Dulness, who is analogous at times in the *Dunciad* to
Venus, the mother of Aeneas:

> But see great Settle to the dust descend,
> And all thy cause and empire at an end!
> Cou'd Troy be sav'd by any single hand,
> His gray-goose-weapon must have made her stand.
>
> (1 185–8)

1. See map, pp. 34–5. A valuable account of the meaning of the City in
the *Dunciad* is given in the EC edition, IV, pp. 24 ff. But the nineteenth-
century editors believed that the 'parodies in the first three books . . . have
little relevancy to the proposed action of the poem'—IV, pp. 21–2.

2. See *Twick. Ed.*, pp. 69–70, note to l. 88.

The lines are a parody of Hector's words when his ghost visits Aeneas in a dream on the night that Troy is sacked by the Grecians:

> Troy nods from high, and totters to her fall . . .
> If by a mortal hand my father's throne
> Could be defended, 't was by mine alone.
> Now Troy to thee commends her future state,
> And gives her gods companions of thy fate.[1]

And so, with the death of Settle (our poetic Hector here[2]), Pope's mythic 'Troy' is doomed. But shortly after this event the mock-Aeneas of the *Dunciad*, Theobald, is whisked away from his 'Troy' by his goddess-mother, and preparations are made for his invasion of the polite world to the west, the poem's 'Latium'. This, in brief, is the 'action' Pope contended that his poem possessed—the translation of an imaginary literary empire from one geographical location to another, the spreading of duncery over a new world not yet 'known' in terms of Dulness's divine sovereignty.

As this 'action' appears in the *Dunciad* it is not rigidly schematized; on the contrary, it is accomplished in a highly allusive manner. It is by the parodying, sometimes merely by the echoing, of certain crucial passages in Virgil's poem, and by the artful disposition of such parodies and echoes in the context of duncery, that Pope has allied, in very allusive but still quite definite terms, the action of the *Aeneid* with the events of his own poem.

A comparison of the propositions of the two poems suggests immediately the relevant connection. Just as Aeneas was the first to bring his gods from Troy to Italy, so Theobald is

1. *Aeneid*, II 384, 387–90 (Dryden's trans.). Pope's parodies of the *Aeneid* in the *Dunciad* contain striking verbal parallels with Dryden's translation. For this reason Dryden's version of the *Aeneid* is employed throughout this chapter, and all line references relating to Virgilian material are to it unless otherwise noted.

2. In Book III of the *Dunciad* Settle appears in the role of Anchises, the father of Aeneas, and conducts his poetical heir, Theobald, on a tour of the underworld. So long as we recognize the portions of the *Aeneid* being parodied in each instance the change in character presents no difficulty.

> the first who brings
> The Smithfield Muses to the Ear of Kings.

The muses, those presiding over the farces and pantomimes, correspond to the Lares transported by Aeneas. Then occur the Invocations, followed by a similar inquiry by both poets as to the 'causes' of the actions they are about to sing, and after this, more important, a parallel which invests the action of the *Dunciad* with Virgilian suggestions of mighty and destined empires. Pope describes the sacred dome of the goddess Dulness:

> This, the Great Mother dearer held than all
> The clubs of Quidnunc's, or her own Guild-hall.
> Here stood her Opium, here she nurs'd her Owls,
> And destin'd here th' imperial seat of Fools.
>
> (I 33–6)

Virgil describes Carthage:

> Carthage the name; belov'd by Juno more
> Than her own Argos, or the Samian shore.
> Here stood her chariot; here, if Heav'n were kind,
> The seat of awful empire she design'd.   (I 23–6)

Pope's source refers to Juno's plans for Carthage, but it is the general context of dominion and empire which is important and which he converts to his own design:

> Hence [from the sacred dome of Dulness] springs each
>   weekly Muse, the living boast
> Of Curl's chaste press, and Lintot's rubric post,
> Hence hymning Tyburn's elegiac lay,
> Hence the soft sing-song on Cecilia's day,
> Sepulchral lyes our holy walls to grace,
> And New-year Odes, and all the Grubstreet race.
>
> (I 37–42)

The above passage is an imitation of these lines in the *Aeneid* relating to the future glories of Rome:

> From whence the race of Alban fathers come,[1]
> And the long glories of majestic Rome.   (I 9–10)

---

1. Pope of course substitutes the 'Grubstreet race' for that of the 'Alban fathers'. The connection between the future empire of Dulness and that of

By recalling two contexts in one extended parody Pope has united what was said about the future of Carthage to what is forecast of Rome. And ultimately both contexts impart their suggestions of imperial destiny to Pope's notion of a future reign of dulness.

With the connection between the future empires of Theobald and Aeneas thus realized, Pope next displays for us the fall of his fictive Troy. Theobald is seen in his study surrounded by his own writings as well as by other monuments to Dulness. This literature of heroic duncery he heaps up for an epic sacrifice, but before setting fire to the pile, Pope's hero bemoans the imminent destruction of Dulness's favourite city in terms drawn largely from Books II and III of the *Aeneid*, where Aeneas relates to Dido the fall of Ilium. Thus, in ll. 183–4, Theobald echoes Anchises' lament at the razing of Troy by saying,

> Had heav'n decreed such works a longer date,
> Heav'n had decreed to spare the Grubstreet-state.

In the original situation Anchises had declared to Aeneas:

> Had Heav'n decreed that I should life enjoy,
> Heav'n had decreed to save unhappy Troy. (II 866–7)

And immediately after this appears the reference to our mock-Hector, Settle, upon whose death will topple the literary Ilium of Pope's poem:

> But see great Settle to the dust descend,
> And all thy cause and empire at an end!
> Cou'd Troy be sav'd by any single hand,
> His gray-goose-weapon must have made her stand.

But it is when Theobald lights the sacrificial pyre erected from his own works that the two empires are yoked most hilariously and ingeniously. First,

---

Aeneas is reinforced a little later in the *Dunciad* by such lines as these:
> Much she [Dulness] revolves their arts, their ancient praise,
> And sure succession down from Heywood's days.   (I 95–6)
The source of this refers to the rulers of Rome who succeed Aeneas:
> And settled sure succession in his line.   (Dryden's trans., I 8)

> he lifted thrice the sparkling brand,
> And thrice he dropt it from his quiv'ring hand:
> Then lights the structure, with averted eyes;
> The rowling smokes involve the sacrifice.[1]   (I 203–6)

Then, in the next lines, with leaping flames and crackling embers, 'Troy' is consumed by fire:

> The opening clouds disclose each work by turns,
> Now flames old Memnon, now Rodrigo burns,
> In one quick flash see Proserpine expire,
> And last, his own cold Æschylus took fire.

What makes the parody so brilliant is the fact that, with the exception of the proper names[2] involved (mainly of classical origin, even they have some auditory appropriateness), Pope's lines could almost be substituted for those by which Dryden describes the conflagration which consumed Troy:

> The palace of Deïphobus ascends
> In smoky flames, and catches on his friends.
> Ucalegon burns next . . .   (II 417–19)

Standing amidst the ruins of his literary empire, Theobald, in a passage which states explicitly the connection the reader should make and recalls all the traditional descriptions of Aeneas as a hero who wept easily,[3] is shown in tears:

> Then gush'd the tears, as from the Trojan's eyes
> When the last blaze sent Ilion to the skies.

At this juncture, like Venus to her son Aeneas, Dulness appears. Dousing the flames with a sheet of Philips' *Thule* (a 'cold' poem), the goddess-mother conveys her son to her sacred dome. The lines are a close parody of Dryden's translation of the Virgil:

1. Each of the lines in this passage is highly suggestive of epic situations. Cf. *Aeneid* (Dryden's trans.), VI 319, VIII 141.
2. 'Memnon', 'Rodrigo', and 'Proserpine' refer to personages who appeared in plays in which Theobald had a hand. 'Aeschylus' refers to a translation of the Greek dramatist proposed by Theobald. See *Twick. Ed.*, pp. 87–8, notes to ll. 208–9, 210.
3. Dryden defends this quality of Aeneas in his *Dedication of the Æneis*.

Pope: Her ample presence fills up all the place;
            A veil of fogs dilates her awful face;
            Great in her charms! as when on Shrieves and May'rs
            She looks, and breathes her self into their airs.
                                                    (I 217-20)

Virgil: Great in her charms, as when on gods above
            She looks, and breathes herself into their love.
                                                    (II 804-5)

Transported to the site from which the new empire will develop,
as Aeneas was aided on his journey to Italy, Theobald is
anointed king, and Book I closes with a prophetic statement
about the extension of his reign over Britain:

> "I see a King! who leads my chosen sons
> To lands, that flow with clenches and with puns:
> 'Till each fam'd Theatre my empire own,
> 'Till Albion, as Hibernia, bless my throne!
> I see! I see!—" Then rapt, she spoke no more.
> "God save King Tibbald!" Grubstreet alleys roar.
>   (I 251-6)

Although the foregoing account may explain what Pope considered to be the 'action' of his poem, there still remains of course
the charge that the hero does nothing: he doesn't have love
affairs or wage epic battles; he merely laments, sleeps, and
dreams. As applied to the *Dunciad*, however, the expectation
that the action should be exhibited in the physical acts of the
hero originates from false assumptions. The first of these is the
assumption that the *Dunciad* is an epic[1]—which indeed it makes
no pretension of being. On only one of its levels of interpretation
is the poem even a parody of epic. Furthermore, critics ignore
the fact that it is only the 'action' of the *Aeneid* to which Pope
compares his poem. There is nothing in the *Dunciad* comparable
to the love of Dido or the conflict with Turnus, for these are the
episodes of Virgil's work, not the action—the 'Removal of the
Empire of Troy to Latium'—as his epic 'Proposition' defines it
for us:

> Arms, and the man I sing, who, forc'd by fate,
> And haughty Juno's unrelenting hate,

1. Highet (*M.L.R.*, 36, p. 331) says 'The *Dunciad* is a bad epic.'

C

> Expell'd and exil'd, left the Trojan shore.
> Long labors, both by sea and land, he bore,
> And in the doubtful war, before he won
> The Latian realm, and built the destin'd town;
> His banish'd gods restor'd to rites divine,
> And settled sure succession in his line,
> From whence the race of Alban fathers come,
> And the long glories of majestic Rome.
>
> (Dryden's trans., I 1–10)

This is the 'action' that Pope has imitated in the establishment of a new empire and 'sure succession' for Dulness, not the entire *Aeneid* part by part.

The difficulty has arisen, perhaps, from a failure to consider what Pope and his contemporaries thought to be the *Aeneid*'s action. Here Le Bossu, certainly an authority in the period, can shed the proper light:

> The *Proposition* should only comprehend the Matter of the Poem; that is, the Action, and the Persons that Act, whether Divine or Humane. We find all this in the *Iliad*, the *Odysseis*, and the *Æneid*.
>
> The Action *Homer* proposes in the *Iliad* is *the Revenge of Achilles*; that of the *Odysseis* is *the Return of Ulysses*; and that of the *Æneid* is *the Empire of* Troy *translated into* Italy *by* Æneas.[1]

The *whole* action, in other words, is the 'Change of a State which is ruin'd at *Troy*, and re-establish'd in *Italy* by *Æneas*'.[2] And the episodes of the poem are, of course, only parts of this whole. The episode in which Dido figures is complete only for her; for Aeneas it 'is only invented to retard the Settlement' in Italy, is only a 'simple Circumstance of an Action [the translation of empire], that is not finish'd'.[3]

Placed in this light, Pope's alliance of the events of his poem with the 'action' of the *Aeneid* can be seen to serve two functions. It supplies a type of 'narrative' progression and structure, and

---

1. *Monsieur Bossu's Treatise of the Epick Poem*, II, pp. 9–10.
  Cf. Addison, *The Spectator*, no. 267: 'Æneas makes his first appearance in the Tyrrhene seas, and within sight of Italy, because the action proposed to be celebrated was that of his settling himself in Latium.'
2. *Monsieur Bossu's Treatise of the Epick Poem*, I, p. 163.
3. Ibid., I, p. 144–5.

it permits a complex interplay of different realms of value. For the moment it is the narrative movement alone which I would consider, particularly that of *Dunciad* I, for it is there that the 'action' of Virgil's poem is imitated in its most sweeping terms: the fall of Troy, the 'removal' of Aeneas from Troy, the inception of the new empire. This movement, as it appears in Book I, can be described as conceptual; that is, it exhibits a progression from one qualitative state (the condition of Theobald amid his literary ruins) to another (Theobald seen as the hero who will carry the Smithfield Muses to the ears of the king in the court world to the west). The parodies of Virgil's epic which we have isolated in *Dunciad* I form a series of guide-posts which direct us along a narrative path through a tangle of satiric and comic scenery. As we move from one significant event to the next, a sense of passage of time and change of place is established. Compared to the miscellaneous parody of epic episodes in the later two books of the *Dunciad*, the events chosen here are rigorously selected; for Pope desires mainly to give the reader an echo of the whole action of the *Aeneid* (the fall of one state and the rise of another) unobscured and uncluttered by parodies which would refer to non-essential episodes or events in Virgil's poem.

It is true that the 'action' Pope imparts to the *Dunciad* does not always serve as a completely successful structural device. The heterogeneous satiric materials tend at times to overwhelm and blur the book's narrative movement. The highly allusive, sometimes oversubtle manner by which the 'action' is realized is not always capable of bringing the poem's materials into a totally satisfactory order. In addition, there are occasions when Pope appears too perfunctory in his handling of events essential to his 'action'. The two lines, for example, which describe the 'removal' of Theobald from his ruined 'Troy' by his goddess-mother,

> She bids him wait her to the sacred Dome;
> Well-pleas'd he enter'd, and confess'd his Home,
>
> (I 221–2)

are too uncircumstantial and flat to reflect adequately the heroic events in the *Aeneid* to which they refer.

The later books of the *Dunciad* (the parody of the epic games in Book II and of the visit to Hades in Book III) nourish and fatten up the epic context, sustain the heroic background, and support the action set forth in Book I. They continue our awareness of the narrative progression: in Book III the vision of the future assures us that

> from Booths to Theatre, to Court,
> Her seat imperial, Dulness shall transport, (301–2)

while Book IV, added in 1743, presents to us the actual fulfilment of the prophecies which forecast a reign of Dulness—the setting of the book is a royal court (presumably that of St James's), and there enthroned are Dulness and her son. This enthronement of Dulness (which is not without its suggestions that George II,[1] as well as Theobald, is to be regarded as king of all duncery) finally brings to completion the 'removal' of the seat of empire from the City to the 'polite world'. The Smithfield Muses have then been brought to the ears of kings.

One other problem relating to the epic narrative which has troubled critics is the character of the goddess Dulness. Highet, for example, calls her a 'miserably thin personification', and adds that 'no one knows who she is meant to be'.[2] This view seems exaggerated. That Dulness plays a role analogous to Venus we have seen already, and she has other affinities which apparently have gone unrecognized. One of these, derived from classical mythology, is a kinship with the Mighty Mother of the Gods, *Magna Mater*, the maternal deity whose cult was popular in Rome and is encountered often in classical literature. Several times in the *Dunciad* Pope's goddess is called the 'Mighty Mother', and a note by the poet to l. 33, Book I, of the 1729 version of the poem says, '*Magna Mater*, here applyed to *Dulness*'.

Magna Mater was historically confused, it is important to note, with other maternal deities such as Berecynthia, Rhea,

1. Cf. the lines,
> Say from what cause, in vain decry'd and curst,
> Still Dunce the second reigns like Dunce the first, (I 5–6)
and Sutherland's comment (*Twick. Ed.*, p. 61, note to l. 6) that 'Pope is probably glancing at George II, who had succeeded his father less than a year before the *Dunciad* was published.'

2. *M.L.R.*, 36, p. 331.

Ceres, Minerva, even Juno and Venus (Aphrodite). Generally she was known, however, by some name which called to mind the land whence she came, Phrygia, and by her connections with the legendary parent city of Rome—Troy.[1] Even more significant for the action of the *Dunciad* is the fact that the removal of the Mighty Mother's statue from the land of Troy to Italy is described by Ovid[2] as the consummation of the Trojan emigration: the goddess had wished to voyage with Aeneas, but the Fates had decreed otherwise. What the Mighty Mother does instead forms the basis of an episode in the *Aeneid*: she gives to Aeneas trees from her native Mount Ida with which to build his ships and intercedes on his behalf before Jove. This tradition, and the fact that Venus could be confused with her, may have suggested her to Pope as the prototype for his goddess, who brings about the consummation of the long-expected reign of dulness.

Since Magna Mater was also known as Berecynthia, one suspects that in the following close imitation of the *Aeneid*, VI 784 ff., Pope is developing that parallel:

> As Berecynthia, while her offspring vye
> In homage, to the mother of the sky,
> Surveys around her in the blest abode
> A hundred sons, and ev'ry son a God:
> Not with less glory mighty Dulness crown'd,
> Shall take thro' Grubstreet her triumphant round,
> And Her Parnassus glancing o'er at once,
> Behold a hundred sons, and each a dunce. (III 123–30)

Likewise, the duncical noise-making contest held in Book II may derive its inspiration from the passage in Ovid's *Fasti* where Magna Mater's predilection for continual noise and the progression of her clamorous priests through the streets is described. Ovid states that the 'Great Goddess delights in perpetual din',[3] and Dulness, who trusts absolutely in the power of noise, sets her sons (who often are called 'priests' in the *Dunciad*) the task of

1. Grant Showerman, *The Great Mother of the Gods*, reprinted from the *Bulletin of the University of Wisconsin*, Philology and Literature Series, vol. 1, no. 3 (Madison, 1901), pp. 296–7.
2. *Fasti*, IV 247–76.   3. IV 191 ff.

seeing who can raise the greatest uproar, and also leads them on a tumultuous progress through the streets of London.[1]

When Pope added Book IV to the *Dunciad* these suggestions of Magna Mater were expanded. There, when the prophecies of a universal reign of Dulness have been fulfilled, Pope's comically maternal goddess celebrates what the poet calls the 'greater Mysteries'. The terms used by Scriblerus in the note to l. 517, Book IV, seem to associate the rites of Dulness with the secret religious rites of pagan antiquity. The justification of the association lies in the fact that it fixes upon Dulness and her sons the suggestion of something obscene and profane. Indeed, any relation of the sons of Dulness to the priests of Magna Mater aids Pope's satiric purpose, for the latter were viewed even by classical writers with contempt and ridicule: they are 'the butt of Martial's obscene wit, and the lash of Juvenal's scorn descends upon the cult again and again'.[2] Considered a noisy, beggarly, contemptible lot by many writers, they are clearly enough analogous to Pope's 'Grubstreet race'.

Since Venus was the mother of Aeneas it may seem that a more straightforward imitation of the Goddess of Love would have been more appropriate to the action of Pope's poem. But the governing deity of the *Dunciad* has obligations to a broader area of meaning in the poem, and too strict a parody of Venus would have narrowed her range of suggestion. Some representative of a principle more primal and more symbolic of wisdom was needed. For this purpose Magna Mater was well qualified, for she was often described as the mother of all creation and being, and had been allegorized by the Emperor Julian as the intelligible principle of the universe.[3] Although Magna Mater could suggest Venus (through the historical confusion we have noted) on the level of epic narrative, an outright imitation of the latter would not have called to mind those qualities in the Mighty Mother which function, as we shall see, on another level of the *Dunciad*'s meaning. Pope has maintained enough ambigu-

1. Book II 213 ff.   2. Showerman, p. 299.
3. *The Works of the Emperor Julian*, trans. by W. C. Wright, The Loeb Classical Library (London, William Heinemann; New York, The Mac-Millan Co., 1913), I 463, 465. The title of Julian's allegory is 'Hymn to the Mother of the Gods'.

ity in his goddess for her to be readily referable either to the Venus of the *Aeneid*, or to the much more complex realm we shall explore later.

III

Only a week before the *Dunciad* was published, there appeared a letter in the *Daily Journal* stating that Pope was writing a poem to be called 'The Progress of Dulness'.[1] Pope attributed the letter to his old enemy John Dennis, but even so there is a possibility that this was actually the title of an earlier version of the *Dunciad*. The information is helpful, for the conception of a 'progress' provides an extremely useful handle with which to grasp certain aspects of the poem. The major narrative progression is of course that movement from 'Troy' to 'Latium' revealed in Book I in terms of the epic metaphor, but Pope has incorporated in each of the later two books other 'progresses' which are auxiliary to the main action. These, while meshing with the general mock-epic pattern, also act as 'stiffening' factors in the poem's over-all design and add to its richness of meaning.

In Book I the idea of a progress from one area of London to another is sometimes obscured by the mass of satiric material with which the poem's 'action' is burdened. There, moreover, the actual 'removal' seems to be the work of an instant: one has the impression that Theobald is rapt away in the cloudy folds of his goddess-mother and set down almost immediately in her sacred dome. But in Book II the movement from one area to another is clearly delineated in a step-by-step, or rather a street-by-street, fashion. The dunces go on a well-defined progress through the streets of London and begin to realize geographically the 'action' Pope claimed for his poem. From their base in the City the powers of duncery conduct an invasion of the polite world in Westminster, and the physical reality of their journey through the streets operates to supply the reader with that tangible suggestion of action, of movement and change, which critics have accused the poem of lacking. In Book II, therefore, contem-

1. See *Twick. Ed.*, p. xvii.

porary London topography is an essential, meaningful part of
the poem. And the progress of the duces through the City and
its environs is more than an artless meandering; it is allied, in
fact, with one of the most ancient civic traditions of London—
the journey of the Lord Mayor of London, on the day that he
takes office, from the City to Westminster.

Pope informs the reader that the

> time and date of the Action [of the *Dunciad*] is evidently in the
> last reign, when the office of City Poet expir'd upon the death
> of *Elkanah Settle*, and he [i.e., Pope] has fix'd it to the Mayoral-
> ty of Sir *Geo. Thorold*.[1]

Further defining the time and occasion are these whimsical
lines describing the events and pageantry of a Lord Mayor's
Day:

> 'Twas on the day, when Thorold, rich and grave,
> Like Cimon triumph'd, both on land and wave:
> (Pomps without guilt, of bloodless swords and maces,
> Glad chains, warm furs, broad banners, and broad faces)
> Now Night descending, the proud scene was o'er,
> But liv'd, in Settle's numbers, one day more.
> Now May'rs and Shrieves all hush'd and satiate lay,
> Yet eat in dreams the custard of the day.   (1 83–90)

Throughout the *Dunciad* the reader is reminded of this traditional celebration, held when the new Lord Mayor took over
the administration of the City.

The path pursued by the duces in their riotous peregrina-
tions about London is markedly similar to that followed by the
Lord Mayor and his attendants in their journey from the City
to Westminster. The pageantry of this civic event, therefore,
takes on metaphoric weight. The Lord Mayor, as the highest
civil authority, easily becomes, however ridiculously described,
the power and affluence of the City personified. He and the City
itself become, in the *Dunciad*, symbolic of certain values—and so
does the court world to the west. The two areas were dedicated,
however, to quite different standards of value, and when, in the
Dunciad, the commercial and middle-class standards of the City

1. Ibid., p. 205.

invade the aristocratic province and corrupt the standards traditionally associated with the king and the nobility, the event is
represented by Pope as a cultural catastrophe. Classical and
humane letters, so long fostered by the aristocracy and bound up
with humanistic ethics and ideals, appear to be threatened in
the *Dunciad* by the combined onslaughts of trading-class attitudes and a debased literary practice.[1]

It is difficult to define precisely the value of the two symbols of
City and Court, but, with a little knowledge of the physical,
social, and economic history of the London area, their general
significance can be grasped. The City itself, comprising the
wards within the old wall and the wards and liberties without,
was set off clearly in the minds of Pope's contemporaries from
the fashionable and court world westward. As a result of the
two-fold disaster of plague and fire in the seventeenth century,
many of the nobility had fled the City never to take up residence
there again. Instead, in the reign of the later Stuarts, there began
the great aristocratic settlement and development of the West
End; the age of the London squares began then, and Covent
Garden, Lincoln's Inn Fields, St James's, Leicester Fields, Red
Lion, Golden, and Soho squares were laid out for the aristocracy. Fearful as they were that overcrowding by the lower
classes might result in a repetition of plague and fire, the nobility
reserved, as much as possible, the western area to themselves.
Even soot played an important part in the division, for with the
increased use of coal, the dust of which was carried eastward by
the prevailing west winds, there was an even more marked distinction between the two regions.[2]

1. The attack by the 'Men of Sense' (writers of a predominantly middle-
class view) on the 'Men of Wit' (writers of an aristocratic turn of mind) that
occurred near the end of the seventeenth century is certainly related to the
imaginative situation in the *Dunciad*. For an account of the earlier quarrel
see the article by Robert M. Krapp, 'Class Analysis of a Literary Controversy: Wit and Sense in Seventeenth Century English Literature', in *Science
and Society*, 10 (1946), pp. 80–92.
2. See Norman G. Brett-James, *The Growth of Stuart London* (London,
George Allen & Unwin Ltd, 1935), pp. 366, 25. See also G. M. Trevelyan,
England Under Queen Anne: Blenheim (London, Longmans, Green & Co.,
1930), p. 80.
John Evelyn wanted all works employing coal moved five miles down the
Thames. See Brett-James, p. 313.

The City and Court were set apart by other circumstances too, some of them going back to the sixteenth century. Strife between the City and the sovereign was an old story, the former constantly and successfully guarding and asserting its liberty and privileges against any encroachment by the latter. It seemed as if those monarchs whom the City favoured invariably prospered, while those whom she opposed 'built for the day' only. Though only two miles away from the Court and Parliament, London was less under their jurisdiction than was any other portion of English soil, and the 'Civil War and the period of the Commonwealth produced a distinct break between the Court and City, which was never healed during the seventeenth century'.[1] In addition, it was in 'the City', as Courthope says, that 'the Whigs found their stronghold, and here were the headquarters of the moneyed interest, so obnoxious to the Tory Party'.[2]

'Political, as well as literary reasons', continues Courthope, 'made the Poet regard the City as the chosen abode of Dulness.' To say that Pope was merely indulging in the conventional and stylish sneer at the London 'cit' in his references to the City inhabitants is to overlook the really sharp and deep-rooted antagonisms which existed, as well as to minimize the values considered by the poet to be at stake.

In the celebration of the Lord Mayor's Day the City Poet had an important role: he composed the poems addressed to the Mayor, designed the various triumphs, and published an account of the festivities in which the floats and dress of the participants were described.[3] From these printed accounts it can be seen that the path followed by the procession was more or less traditional. Starting at Guildhall, it usually proceeded down King Street to Three-Crane Wharf; from there the Mayor and his immediate party travelled by barge to Westminster Hall to

1. Trevelyan, pp. 75, 72. Brett-James, p. 366.

2. EC, IV, pp. 24–5. Courthope seems to have grasped better than any editor before or after him the significance of much that is discussed here, yet he continually stopped short of the connections and conclusions I am attempting to present.

3. Frederick W. Fairholt, in *Lord Mayor's Pageants* (London, 1843), reprints several of these accounts, and many others survive.

receive the oath of office, returning by water again to Black-Friars Landing; thence the procession moved back up into the City by various routes, but usually through Ludgate.[1] Since the Lord Mayor's procession journeyed from that symbol of City interest, Guildhall, to the world of the court represented by Westminster Hall, this progress could be seen by Pope as offering an analogy to the spreading influence of dulness, the translation of empire, the deterioration in art and morals, that his poem postulated.

The correspondence between the progress of the dunces and the progress of the Lord Mayor's procession through the streets is not exact, but there are many remarkable similarities in the routes followed by the two processions. There are those occasions when the dunces diverge from the path followed by the Lord Mayor; but even the divergences appear to realize, in symbolic fashion, the mayoral journey. Pope, for whatever reason, has sacrificed historical accuracy in certain respects, but the imaginative significance of the geographical movements in the poem remains clear. Thus one may find fault with details in Pope's design, or regard certain correspondences between the progress of Dulness and that of the Lord Mayor as being inadequately realized, yet the total context of the poem—its setting of a particular Lord Mayor's Day, the numerous references to the mayoral pageantry, the precision with which the poet designates the geographic location of various events and movements —would appear to support an attempt to make sense out of the similarities which obviously do exist.

After a night spent at the sacred dome of Dulness near the Tower of London,[2] the goddess and the dunces move through the City to the site of St Mary le Strand church in the Strand, just beyond the western boundary of the City, that is, just beyond the ward of Farringdon Without and Temple Bar.[3] The spot is highly significant, for at the Strand began the jurisdiction

1. This movement can be followed easily on the map, pp. 34–5.
2. The time sequence is given by Pope in the note to l. 258, Book II. See *Twick. Ed.*, p. 133. According to Pope's note to l. 27, Book I (*Twick Ed.*, p. 63), the sacred dome of Dulness is located at Rag Fair, 'a place near the *Tower of London*, where old cloaths and frippery are sold'.
3. The 'bars' marked off the City limits outside the wall.

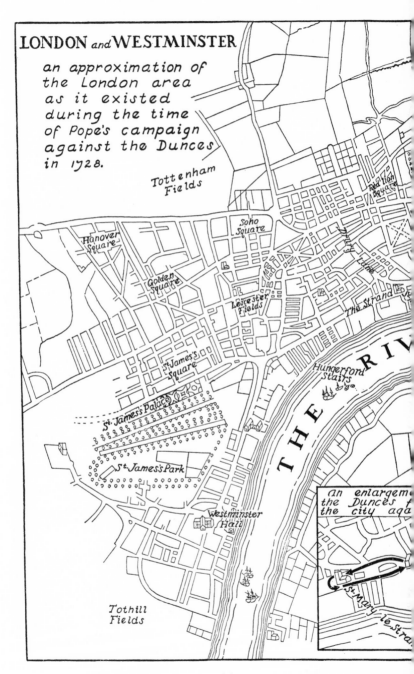

LONDON *and* WESTMINSTER

an approximation of
the London area
as it existed
during the time
of Pope's campaign
against the Dunces
in 1728.

Tottenham
Fields

Red Lion
Square

Soho
Square

Drury Lane

Hanover
Square

Golden
Square

Leicester
Fields

The Strand

St James's
Square

Hungerford
Stairs

St James's Palace

THE RIV

St James's Park

an enlargem
the Dunces t
the city aqa

Westminster
Hall

St Mary le Stra

Tothill
Fields

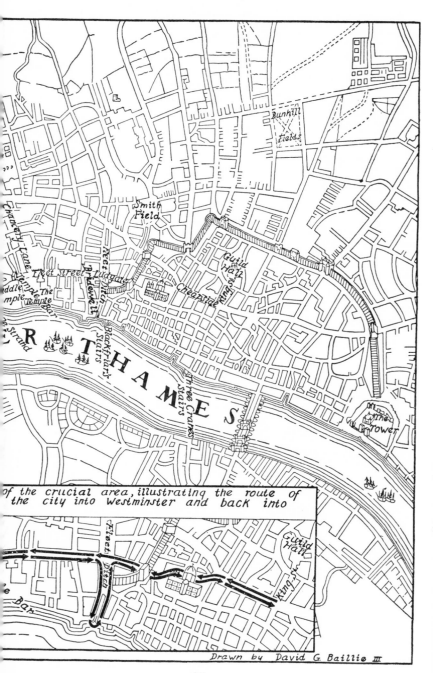

of Westminster. It is also important that, historically, there were
two ways by which the mayor journeyed from London to Westminster—'one by the river and the other along the Strand'.[1] It
probably would have been difficult for Pope to take his dunces
on the more customary river voyage; he appears instead to have
designed the procession of the duncesinto the Strand to recall
past mayoral journeys to Westminster via the land route.

Then, where Drury Lane enters the Strand, the dunces engage in their ludicrous parody of the epic games. The exact geo-
graphy of the games seems partly determined by the fact that
the Strand and Drury Lane were the actual sites of many print-
ing-houses and theatres, and so could mark the encroachment of
literary dulness on Westminster.

It is the last of the epic exercises held at this spot, the noise-
making contest in which Sir Richard Blackmore is victor, that is
particularly important. Faced westward in the Strand (the
major thoroughfare leading directly towards St James's palace)
Blackmore's long, far-reaching howl moves on a very well-
defined progress:

> But far o'er all, sonorous Blackmore's strain,
> Walls, steeples, skies, bray back to him again:
> In Tot'nam fields, the brethren[2] with amaze
> Prick all their ears up, and forget to graze;
> Long Chanc'ry-lane retentive rolls the sound,
> And courts to courts return it round and round:
> Thames wafts it thence to Rufus' roaring hall,
> And Hungerford re-ecchoes, bawl for bawl.
> All hail him victor in both gifts of Song,
> Who sings so loudly, and who sings so long.
>
> (II 247–56)

1. Robert Withington, *English Pageantry* (Cambridge, Mass., Harvard
University Press, 1918, 1920), II, p. 4. The land procession was customary
until the fifteenth century. I have been unable to learn how often the journey by land was made after that time. Withington reprints (II, pp. 89–91) an
excellent description, written about 1740, of a Lord Mayor's Day. The
account reveals clearly the exact geographical route of one such procession
in Pope's time.

2. The 'brethren' donkeys may hint at Puritan preaching, noted for its
'sonorous' qualities. This would suggest again, of course, that Blackmore's
voice is merely the metaphoric vehicle for the spread of middle-class values
westward.

A glance at the map of eighteenth-century London will reveal that the places echoing back Blackmore's 'song' constitute clear boundary markers for the court world, the fashionable districts to the west of the City.[1] This area was bounded by Tottenham Fields to the north, by Westminster Hall (called 'Rufus' roaring hall' in the poem) and the Thames on the south and south-east. For the eastern boundary Pope uses Chancery Lane, and it can be seen from the map that this is the *only* major thoroughfare he could have used to separate the City of London from the City of Westminster. Hungerford Stairs at the bend of the river serves to channel the sound of Blackmore's bawl in the most significant direction; there was no point in making the sound go south of the river, an area that was largely under City jurisdiction and in-fluence already. Sir Edward Hungerford, moreover, had erected near the river a market, which resulted in an extension of the commercial itch westward:[2]

> influenced by the same motives that prompted his illustrious Eastern neighbours [the City tradesmen], [he] determined to sacrifice the honours of his ancestors, at the shrine of Plutus; and obtained an act in the reign of Charles II. to make leases of the site of his mansion and grounds, where a market was soon after erected . . .[3]

That Pope carefully selected the boundaries of Blackmore's stentorian bray is indicated by a textual change which has troubled critics.[4] A manuscript reading has 'Tothill fields', a place in southern Westminster, instead of 'Tot'nham Fields', the area to the north of Westminster. The explanation of the

1. Pope re-emphasizes the progress in a note to l. 250, Book II (*Twick. Ed.*, p. 130), stating he has imitated the voice of Virgil's Alecto, that hellish sound at which mothers clutched their children to their breasts (*Aeneid*, VII 516 ff.).
Courthope specifies some of these places to mark off the West End, with-out—oddly enough—connecting them with Blackmore's voice and its travels. They are practically inescapable boundaries for any description of Westminster in Pope's time.
2. There were many such signs of City encroachment upon the West End. The palaces along the Strand had given way by Pope's time to streets of houses (Brett-James, p. 366), and to publishing concerns.
3. J. P. Malcolm, *Londinium Redivivum* (London, 1807), IV, p. 308.
4. See *Twick. Ed.*, p. 130, note to l. 249.

change would seem to be that, with the southern limit already set by Westminster Hall, Pope needed a northern boundary. In the revised passage, the whole area westward between Tottenham Fields and Westminster Hall is subdued by the lung power of Blackmore.

The selection of Sir Richard Blackmore as the 'voice' of the City powers is important, for the poetically prolific physician had been dubbed the 'City Knight', the 'City Bard', the 'Cheapside Poet'. The 'pious' and 'decent' defender and promoter of middle-class *mores*, he was a most appropriate agent for the extension of City standards into the court world.[1] Representative in the *Dunciad* of poetic folly and bourgeois morality, he drowns in noise the only area from which any resistance to the reign of Dulness might originate: 'sound', in Oldmixon's words, is imaged as having 'got the better of Sense'; the sphere of order and right reason is seen as overwhelmed by 'empty words' and 'sounding strain'.[2]

Immediately after Blackmore's fearsome accomplishment the dunces follow closely the path of the Lord Mayor's progress. From the Strand (in Westminster) they return to the junction of Fleet-ditch and the Thames, and there hold the mud-diving contest. At this stage there occurs a remarkable coincidence: even the time of day apparently coincides with the hour the Lord Mayor sets out for the river. In a significant note to these lines,

> This labour past, by Bridewell all descend,
> (As morning-pray'r and flagellation end.)
> To where Fleet-ditch with disemboguing streams
> Rolls the large tribute of dead dogs to Thames, (II 257–60)

Pope remarks:

> It is between eleven and twelve in the morning . . . that the criminals are whipp'd in *Bridewell*.—This is to mark punctually the Time of the day: *Homer* does it by the circumstance of

1. See Richard C. Boys, 'Sir Richard Blackmore and the Wits', no. 13 of The University of Michigan Contributions in Modern Philology (Ann Arbor, University of Michigan Press, 1949). See also Robert M. Krapp, *Science and Society*, 10 (1946), pp. 91–2.
2. *Dunciad*, II 41.

the Judges rising from court, or of the Labourer's dinner; our author by one very proper both to the *Persons* and the *Scene* of his Poem; which we may remember commenc'd in the evening of the Lord-Mayor's day: The first book passed in that night; the next morning the games begin in the *Strand*, thence along *Fleetstreet* (places inhabited by Booksellers) then they proceed by *Bridewell* toward *Fleetditch*, and lastly thro' *Ludgate* to the City and the Temple of the Goddess.[1]

And 'between eleven and twelve' was apparently the time at which the Lord Mayor customarily journeyed to the Thames. A passage in the *Gentleman's Magazine* relates that

by eleven o'clock the windows from Black-Friars-bridge,[2] to the north end of King-street, began to exhibit such a number of angelic faces . . . At twenty minutes past eleven the Lord-Mayor left the Hall,[3] being preceded by the city sword and mace, and followed by the Alderman and Sheriffs.[4]

Having voyaged to Westminster, the Lord Mayor then returned to Black-Friars Wharf,[5] a landing immediately adjacent to where Fleet-ditch entered the Thames. And when the dunces have completed their muddy sport at this point, they proceed up from the river along the course taken by the mayoral party after its debarkation close by: they move, that is, with their Goddess up the Fleet and Ludgate Hill, through Ludgate[6] and into the City. Here is a description of the Lord Mayor's route into the City:

Those that went not to Westminster, viz. the pensioners and banners, being set in order, ready to march, the foot marshall in the rere of the artillery company, leads the way along the channel [Fleet-ditch] up Ludgate-Hill, through Ludgate into

1. See *Twick. Ed.*, p. 133, note to l. 258. I have quoted the note at length to indicate the way Pope emphasizes the geographical progress and its connection with the Lord Mayor's festival.
2. Not yet built in 1728.   3. Guildhall.
4. Volume XLIII (1733), p. 577.
5. Fairholt, *Lord Mayor's Pageants*, I, p. 144, n.
6. This is made clearer in the *Greater Dunciad* of 1743 (see *Twick. Ed.*,
p. 315, ll. 359–60):
        Thro' Lud's fam'd gates, along the well-known Fleet
        Rolls the black troop . . .

D

St. Paul's churchyard, and so into Cheapside, where his Lordship is entertained by the first scene or pageant.[1]

Pope's imitation of the 'action' of the *Aeneid* in Book I and the carefully identified geographical movement of Book II work together in the *Dunciad* to suggest the conquest of a 'world' by duncery. And there are other circumstances which further a fusion of the epic and geographical metaphors. England, after all, had a mythical history stretching back to Brute, a descendant of Aeneas. London was Troy-novant, and in many of the mayoral celebrations these Trojan origins were apparently a prominent theme. In the person of Settle, moreover, the epic and civic metaphors again are fused: he was the last City Poet to have charge of the annual mayoral festivities, and in Book III of the *Dunciad* he plays the role of Anchises; he is represented as the father of Pope's fictive Aeneas, Theobald. On Settle's death one empire ('Troy', or the City) of Dulness is 'destroyed', but then his poetical heir undertakes, with the help of the goddess, to establish another and larger empire of the same general character as the old.

We must not overlook the real nature of Pope's achievement in his treatment of City personalities, public buildings, current customs, the 'art' of Settle, Guildhall, George Thorold, allegorical tableaux,[2] the whole clutter of the age's official symbols. For all have been imbued with a quality which transcends their historic or factual significance. It is this process, one by which the local and contemporary, the literary and the personal, become serious metaphoric vehicles, that is central to the *Dunciad*. The tendency of many Augustans to view artistic trifling and decay as symptomatic of fundamental national disorders and weaknesses becomes, in Pope's hands, a highly subtle poetic technique: the debased literature of the dunces and the patronage of such literature by the nobility become the tokens for more profound failings. Order was still thought the first law of heaven, and the wearer of the crown yet regarded as that law's noblest symbol and support. When, in the *Dunciad*, the king and his

1. Fairholt, II, p. 153. Cf. also Withington, *English Pageantry*, II, p. 91.
2. Ll. 43–52 of Book I of the *Dunciad* are evidently a glance at these allegorical tableaux of the pageantry. Cf. *Twick. Ed.*, note to I 44.

nobility, the intellectual and moral preceptors of the nation, give ear to the 'voices' of a Blackmore, a Theobald, or a Cibber, and acquiesce in an invasion of the polite world by writers who pander to flaccid emotions and effeminate minds, their acts (not wholly fictional) become metaphors which suggest a general social and moral breakdown within the nation.

CHAPTER II

THE DUNCIAD OF 1728
(continued)

I

SO veined are Books I and II with metaphors of 'progress' that it is hardly surprising to find that Book III of the *Dunciad* develops the same theme even further, absorbing in this fashion still other ideas and images of artistic and moral decline into the poem's complex design. Thus when Theobald in Book III visits the underworld of Dulness (as Aeneas journeys to Hades), he is given a vision of the future glories to be attained by a race cast in his own heroic mould, a vision which adheres closely to one of the most wide-spread artistic conventions of the seventeenth and eighteenth centuries—the 'progress piece'.[1]

The method of development employed in the traditional progress poem is that of a historical survey of the past. Conscious as they were of being heirs to the mighty civilizations of Greece and Rome, the Augustans never seemed to tire of setting forth for themselves a poetic genealogy which displayed the ultimate classical derivation of their arts and learning. Literally scores of poems were composed in this vein;[2] the titles of such different

1. The 'progress' piece historically may have its origin in the very episode, the vision of the future awarded Aeneas, which Pope is parodying (cf. Dryden's trans., VI 1073 ff.). Pope's use of the convention is also influenced by the prospect of the future awarded Adam in Books XI and XII of *Paradise Lost*. Gilbert Wakefield, *Observations on Pope* (London, 1796), p. 323, prints a manuscript note to *Dunciad* III 334, which speaks of 'the prospective vision, in which these great changes are displayed'. 'Progress' and 'prospect' genres seem to coalesce in *Dunciad* III.

The convention continued to appeal to poets well into the eighteenth century. Gray's 'Progress of Poesy' (1757) is one of the most famous progress pieces.

2. R. H. Griffith has an extensive, but still incomplete, list of 'progress pieces' in his article, 'The Progress Pieces of the Eighteenth Century', *The Texas Review*, 5 (1919–20), pp. 218–33. Additional information is supplied by Mattie Swayne in 'The Progress Piece of the Seventeenth Century', *The University of Texas Bulletin, Studies in English*, 16 (1936), pp. 84–92. My evaluation of the source of the convention, as well as of the sensibility expressed by it, differs from the accounts of these two writers.

works as Dryden's 'Discourse concerning the Original and Progress of Satire' and Hogarth's 'The Rake's Progress' reflect the
preoccupation of the period with the convention, and we have
already remarked upon the fact that the *Dunciad* itself may once
have been called 'The Progress of Dulness'.

As soon as Theobald has encountered his ghostly father
(Settle, in the role of Anchises) in the underworld of Book III, the
latter conducts Pope's mock-Aeneas to a hilltop,

> whose cloudy point commands
> Her [Dulness'] boundless Empire over seas and lands,
> (III 59–60)

and says:

> Far Eastward cast thine eye, from whence the Sun
> And orient Science at a birth begun.   (III 65–6)

Together father and son then witness in a vision[1] the dark cloud
of Dulness which, rising in the East, spreads over the entire
globe. This panoramic envelopment of the earth by dulness and
darkness in successive stages is the portion of Book III which re-
flects the 'progress' convention, and it is to this that Pope refers
when he says that 'the third book, if well consider'd, seemeth to
embrace the whole world'.[2] Rising in China, the shadows cover
Egypt, Rome, Spain, Gaul, Arabia, and finally move toward
Britain. Settle says,

> And see! my son, the hour is on its way,
> That lifts our Goddess to imperial sway:
> This fav'rite Isle, long sever'd from her reign,
> Dove-like, she gathers to her wings again. (III 115–18)

The really important element in Pope's progress piece is its
association with ideas of a historic and geographical continuity
of arts and learning (far too many of the Augustan poems of this
nature deteriorated to an account of the progress of a 'Harlot',
of 'Drink', or of 'Patriotism'[3]). It is the historic consciousness of
his place at the end of a long chronicle of events that underlies

1. Theobald's 'mental eye' is endowed, as are the eyes of Adam in *P.L.*,
XI 411–16, with special powers to enable him to view the future.
2. *Twick. Ed.*, p. 51.   3. Cf. Griffith, *TR*, 5, pp. 230–1.

Pope's use of the convention, an awareness of a great cultural stream which has transmitted to the present the learning of the past.

This is what characterizes also one of the earliest of the progress pieces, Sir John Denham's 'The Progress of Learning'. Beginning with the knowledge infused into Adam by God, Denham pursues this 'learning' through Chaldea, Egypt, Greece, to Italy, from whence, in the wake of Rome's conquering eagles, 'Arts, Learning, and Civility were spread'. And Sir William Temple had expressed his awareness of cultural continuity in very similar fashion:

> Science and Arts have run their circles, and had their periods in the several Parts of the World. They are generally agreed to have held their course from *East* to *West*, to have begun in *Chaldaea* and *Ægypt*, to have been Transplanted from thence to *Greece*, from *Greece* to *Rome*, to have sunk there, and after many Ages to have revived from those Ashes, and to have sprung up again, both in *Italy* and other more *Western* Provinces of *Europe*. When *Chaldaea* and *Ægypt* were Learned and Civil, *Greece* and *Rome* were as rude and barbarous as all *Ægypt* and *Syria* now are and have been long. When *Greece* and *Rome* were at their heights in Arts and Science, *Gaul*, *Germany*, *Britain* were as ignorant and barbarous as any Parts of *Greece* or *Turkey* can be now.[1]

There have been several theories advanced to account for the sudden appearance of the progress piece in the seventeenth century,[2] all of which overlook, it seems to me, the true source and nature of the convention. So far as Denham's version is concerned, at any rate, there can be little doubt of its ultimate derivation from the medieval and renaissance idea of *translatio studii*, the idea of a transplantation from age to age and from country to country of cultural treasure. 'The Progress of Learning' parallels almost exactly an expression of this historic theme found in a sermon uttered before the French king in 1405. Just as Denham's poem traces 'knowledge' back to Adam in Para-

---

1. 'An Essay Upon Ancient and Modern Learning', in *Critical Essays of the Seventeenth Century*, ed. J. E. Spingarn (Oxford, Clarendon Press, 1909), I, pp. 50–1.   2. Cf. Swayne, pp. 84 ff.

dise, from there to the 'Father of the faithful', Abraham, living
in Chaldea, from there to Egypt, from Egypt to Greece, from
Greece to Rome, so

> *Dans son sermon* Vive le Roi! *prononcé pour l'Université devant le
> roi Charles VI, le 7 novembre 1405, renchérissant encore sur ce thème
> [of translatio studii], Jean Gerson fera remonter le savoir au premier
> homme, dans le Paradis Terrestre, d'où il est venu, per successum,
> aux Hébreux; des Hébreux, comme l'écrit Josèphe, aux Egyptiens par
> Abraham; puis d'Egypte à Athènes, d'Athènes à Rome, et enfin de
> Rome à Paris.*[1]

Just as the oft-quoted expression 'we are Dwarfs . . . though we
stand upon a Gyant's shoulders'[2] has a history going back to
Bernard of Chartres, so the idea of a 'transfer of studies' seems to
have persisted from the ninth century (the time of the Carolingian renaissance) onwards. The two metaphors are, moreover,
expressive of similar historical perspectives;[3] both are used by
the 'ancient' party—which included Temple and Pope among
its adherents—to counter the tendency of the 'moderns' to deny
(at least partly) their own place in a continuous tradition going
back to Greece and Rome. The 'moderns', not Pope, wished to
be independent of the past.

Dryden touches faintly on the *translatio studii* in his compli-
mentary epistle 'To the Earl of Roscommon, on His Excellent
Essay on Translated Verse'. A good portion of the poem is concerned with the progress of rhyme, and its opening lines illustrate the typical 'progress' procedure:

> Whether the fruitful Nile, or Tyrian shore,
> The seeds of arts and infant science bore,[4]
> 'T is sure the noble plant, *translated* first,
> Advanc'd its head in Grecian gardens nurs'd.
> The Grecians added verse; their tuneful tongue

1. Étienne Gilson, *La Philosophie Au Moyen Age* (Paris, Payot, 1947), p. 194.
In the chapter entitled 'La Transmission de la Culture Latine', Gilson gives
the best account of the theme of *translatio studii* that I know of. Cf. pp. 193 ff.
2. These are Temple's words. See Spingarn, III, p. 48.
3. Cf. Marcus A. Haworth, 'The *Translatio Studii* in the Carolingian
Renaissance', *The Classical Bulletin*, 26, no. 5 (March 1950), p. 52.
4. Cf. Pope's account of the progress of Dulness:
    (The soil that arts and infant letters bore).   (III 88)

Made nature first and nature's God their song.
Nor stopp'd *translation* here; for conquering Rome
With Grecian spoils brought Grecian numbers home.[1]

Though Dryden is obviously playing on the notion of *linguistic translation*, it seems fairly clear that he is in direct contact with the idea of *translatio studii* as well, the 'translation of studies'. A similar conclusion seems valid for the passage quoted from Temple, for he speaks of arts and sciences as 'Transplanted' from Egypt to Greece, from Greece to Rome, and so on.

It is not that we shall find the actual phrase, *translatio studii*, in the mouths of Pope and his contemporaries. The idea has been expressed at different times in a variety of ways.[2] It is the term's content, its value as a summary statement of a historical perspective, which is of importance here. Like the men of the Carolingian renaissance, the Augustans (at least some of them) saw themselves as heirs to a great and glorious tradition, and their cognizance of this cultural succession has found, perhaps, its most polished expression in Part III of Pope's *Essay on Criticism*. But the Augustans were also afraid of losing the tradition they had inherited; it was conceivable to many that a new 'Gothic invasion' of learning might occur, that the classical ideals and principles might give way before a debased literature, a 'universal depravation of taste', a 'general neglect of letters'. Temple had stated that one glorious centre of culture arose, passed on the torch of learning, and then subsided back into the night of barbarism: it was conceivable that Britain might suffer the same fate, and this becomes an imaginative fact in the *Dunciad*. Against the traditional concept of cultural succession from Greece to Britain, Pope poses a heritage of Dulness, a progress westward of the forces of disorder and darkness. Instead of

1. Ll. 1–8; italics mine.
2. Cf. Haworth, *The Classical Bulletin*, 26, p. 52. My attention was first called to the idea of *translatio studii* by Marshall McLuhan in his unpublished doctoral dissertation, 'The Place of Thomas Nashe in the Learning of His Time', submitted to Cambridge University in 1943. Mr McLuhan at one point suggests that Nashe may be 'alluding to the old tradition of *translatio studii* in speaking of Art as a "banisht Queene into this barraine soile, having monarchized it so long amongst the Greeks and Romanes".' Cf. Nashe's *Works*, ed. R. B. McKerrow (London, Sidgwick & Jackson Ltd, 1910), I, p. 317.

a *translatio studii* we have what we may call a *translatio stultitiae*,
a transplantation of the rule of Dulness to one country after another. Just as, on the level of metaphor, the light of the sun is
eclipsed by the forces of darkness—

> How little, mark! that portion of the ball,
> Where, faint at best, the beams of Science fall—
>
> (III 75–6)

so the accumulated wisdom of the ages is erased by the powers of
Dulness:

> See, the bold Ostrogoths on Latium fall;
> See, the fierce Visigoths on Spain and Gaul.
> See, where the Morning gilds the palmy shore,
> (The soil that arts and infant letters bore)
> His conqu'ring tribes th' Arabian prophet draws,
> And saving Ignorance enthrones by Laws.
> See Christians, Jews, one heavy sabbath keep;
> And all the Western World believe and sleep.
>
> (III 85–92)

The last two lines of the passage allude to another 'progress'
context, that of Dryden's poem 'To Sir Godfrey Kneller':

> Long time the sister arts, in iron sleep,
> A heavy sabbath did supinely keep.   (57–8)

And in Pope's entire narration of the progress of Dulness
through history one is continually conscious of overtones of the
poems of Dryden and Denham I have cited. Put thus in the guise
of habitual statements[1] concerning the transmission of learning

1. How closely Pope's progress of Dulness over the earth conforms to the
concept of *translatio studii* can be seen easily if lines 65–112 of *Dunciad* III are
compared to this statement of the historic theme by an English humanist of
the fourteenth century, Richard de Bury: 'Admirable Minerva seems to
bend her course to all the nations of the earth, and reacheth from end to end
mightily, that she may reveal herself to all mankind. We see that she has
already visited the Indians, the Babylonians, the Egyptians and Greeks, the
Arabs and the Romans. Now she has passed by Paris, and now has happily
come to Britain, the most noble of islands, nay, rather a microcosm in itself,
that she may show herself a debtor both to the Greeks and to the Barbarians.'
—*The Philobiblon of Richard de Bury*, ed. and trans. by E. C. Thomas (London, 1888), p. 212.
   Pope's Dulness, as we shall see, is the opposite of Wisdom (de Bury's
Minerva).

from the past to the present, the movement of Dulness over the world becomes a vivid emblem of the destructive capacity of Pope's dark Goddess—one is faced with the shocking reversal of a historical perspective precious to the Augustans. Furthermore, the very fact that Pope employs so often in his poem the concept of a 'progress'—from the City to the Court, from Heywood to Theobald,[1] from Rome to Augustan London—should indicate to us that Dulness is not something static, a harmless stupidity. Here, out of a minor poetic convention and a most traditional view of history, the poet has created a powerful image of Dulness as an active, expanding, devitalizing force in human affairs.

II

For a long time before Pope compelled the duplicates to go through a 'hollow, mean imitation of the heroic ritual of the epic',[2] many of them had themselves engaged in literary mock-heroics, had paraded their hollow and mean imitations of the ancient heroic poets.[3] And since this aping of classic writings was so prevalent among the dunces, no more fitting punishment could have been devised for them than that by which they are forced to continue, in the timeless realm of art, their emulation of the epic figures of the past: a Theobald in the role of Aeneas, a Settle cast as an Anchises, a Ward as a Marcellus.[4] There is, through Pope's use of parody, at least poetic justice in the situation of the dunces.

In the world of the *Dunciad* one becomes increasingly aware of two opposed realms of value, the classical and the contemporary, the epical and the duncical, each of which exists in tension

1. See Book I 93–106.
2. Geoffrey Tillotson, *On the Poetry of Pope*, p. 55.
3. In his prolific enterprises Blackmore had attempted to draw a Virgilian bow. That what he intended as quite serious heroic poetry might be regarded as only a parody of true epic is suggested by Walter Harte:

> In Works like these [the *Dunciad*] if *Fustian* might appear,
> Mock-Epics, *Blackmore*, would not cost thee dear.

The lines are from Harte's *An Essay on Satire, particularly on the Dunciad*, printed in 1730, and included in Richard Savage's *A Collection of Pieces in Verse and Prose, Which have been publish'd on Occasion of the DUNCIAD* (London, 1732). See p. 12 of Harte's poem in Savage's collection.
4. See ll. 135 ff., Book III.

with the other. These realms, however divergent, are yoked in the poem by Pope's use of parody, and the result is a highly exciting process of action and reaction, assertion and counter-assertion. At one moment, so strong are they in their Pope-given attributes of dulness, the duncos appear about to overwhelm, to sully indelibly, the classical material; in the next, the sublimity of the past functions to devalue completely the activities of the present. This constant alternation is possible because parody can be made to include its model within itself. Pope's mock-epic does not merely refer the reader to the *Aeneid*: the meaning, the classical values attached to Virgil's poem (or to the other classical sources parodied by Pope), become incorporated into the context of the imitation. It is as if one is unable to read Pope without reading Virgil, Horace, and Ovid at the same time, as if every image is a type of double exposure figuring not only dunces, but also epic heroes. In this way, the *Aeneid* and the other classical models are not, finally, outside Pope's poem; they are recreated within it.

The witty interplay of contexts established by the parody in the *Dunciad* results in a multiplicity of rich and varied effects. There is first of all, of course, the pleasure one receives from discovering the familiar in a new context, and the feeling of surprise that it could have been so adapted. At the same time the epic values introduced by the parody may function to produce a humorous reciprocation between the sublime and the ridiculous, or to establish a standard of values by which the duncos may be measured and found wanting: the comparison of a dunce to an Aeneas results, because of the immediately apparent discrepancy between the two, in an elucidation of the one by the other, in a value judgement on the part of the reader. And by this last procedure a system of internal controls is created in the *Dunciad*: by careful selection of his classical contexts, Pope continually modulates or intensifies the evaluative pressure of his material. Ultimately, moreover, this 'governing' process may act to 'distance' the satire. The very variety of the allusions, the array of classical authorities, introduced by Pope into his poem begins to include within its imaginative framework an impersonal standard of judgement. The duncos appear devalued not so much by Pope as by Homer, Virgil, Horace, Ovid: a type of historical perspective on duncery is established as the poem begins to suggest that the dunces have affinities with, for example, the inept and irresponsible writers condemned by Horace.[1]

It was by an almost thematic parody of two quite specific classical *loci*, however, that Pope obtained one of his most sweeping and withering devaluations of the dunces and the age in which they were able to prosper, the England of the first two Georges. The reigns of these monarchs, like those of their predecessors, had been hailed by poets as a return to Saturnian days, a restoration of the Golden Age. But this time the hailing was done mainly by bad poets. The passages most often drawn on were either Virgil's Fourth Eclogue or these lines from the sixth *Aeneid*:

> *hic vir, hic est, tibi quem promitti saepius audis,*
> *Augustus Caesar, Divi genus, aurea condet*
> *saecula qui rursus Latio regnata per arva*
> *Saturno quondam . . .*[2]

And the general temper of the adulation may be gathered from a typical specimen by Eusden:

> *Britain!* un-envious view th' *Italian* Plains!
> See *Rome*'s blest Times restor'd—Thy own
>   AUGUSTUS reigns![3]

1. On two occasions in the *Dunciad* (1 71–2, III 241–2) the reader is reminded of the celebrated opening of Horace's 'Epistle to the Pisos'. There, it will be recalled, Horace expresses his disgust with poets who produce careless and tumid writings.

2. In the Loeb Classical Library edition of Virgil, trans. by H. R. Fairclough (Cambridge, Mass., Harvard University Press; London, William Heinemann Ltd, 1947), the lines are translated thus: 'This, this is he, whom thou so oft hearest promised to thee, Augustus Caesar, son of a god, who shall again set up the Golden Age in Latium amid the fields where Saturn once reigned.'—VI 791–4.
Welsted used such lines, or these from Eclogue IV,
> *Jam nova progenies caelo demittitur alto . . .*
> *Adgredere o magnos (aderit jam tempus) honores,*
> *Cara deum suboles,*   (ll. 7, 48–9)
for the mottoes to his poems in honour of the Hanoverians. See Welsted's *Works, in Verse and Prose* (London, 1787), particularly 'An Epistle to Mr. Steele, on the Kings Accession to the Crown, 1714', and 'A Poem to her Royal Highness the Princess of Wales. . .'

3. See Eclogue IV 10: '*tuus iam regnat Apollo*'.

With an AUGUSTUS may new *Virgils* rise,
And sing the Favourite of conspiring Skies!
To *Albion* Thou (if Poets can presage)
Shalt give another, sweeter, Classic Age![1]

As the duces applied such contexts to the Kings of England,
Pope applies them to his monarch of Dulness. As flattering poets
foretold a Saturnian age, Pope, less flattering, foretold one too.
Thus near the end of Book III the obeisance that Virgil had given
to Augustus, and the duces to George, is passed on to Theobald:

Now Bavius, take the poppy from thy brow,
And place it here! here all ye Heroes bow!
This, this is He, foretold by ancient rhymes,
Th' Augustus born to bring Saturnian times:
Beneath his reign, shall Eusden wear the bays,
Cibber preside Lord-Chancellor of Plays,
B[enson] sole Judge of Architecture sit,
And Namby Pamby[2] be prefer'd for Wit! (III 315–22)

Eusden had foretold the rise of 'new Virgils' under George II;
Pope also forecasts another 'sweeter, Classic Age', but one marked by the rise of such 'court poets' as Eusden himself, Colley
Cibber, and Ambrose Philips. As used by the duces, the classical references—the value terms like 'Rome', 'Augustus', 'Mae-
cenas'—have been emptied of meaning; Pope's use of the same
terms[3] to refer to the duces themselves reveals how completely disproportionate the terms are when applied to the British
Caesars. It is suggested that what is said of George, King of England, can as well be said of Theobald, King of Dulness, and vice
versa. By the irony of the honorific language[4] contemporary

1. Lawrence Eusden, *Three Poems* (London, 1727). Cf. 'A Poem, on the
happy Succession, and Coronation of His present Majesty', p. 11.

2. Namby Pamby was a name given to Ambrose Philips because of certain
qualities of his verse.

3. The lines describing Berecynthia, the mighty mother, gazing around at
her hundred sons (cf. *Dunciad*, III 123–30), were sometimes used in regard to
the Queens of England, the 'mothers' of the land. See John Bancks, *Miscellaneous Works, in Verse and Prose* (London, 1738), II, p. 156. The reference
occurs in a poem entitled 'The Royal Guardian'.

4. The comments of Maynard Mack, *Pope and His Contemporaries*, p. 34,
should be read in connection with this discussion. Pope's 'Epistle to Augustus' is another example of the technique here discussed.

England is made to appear as a feeble parody of an age in the
heroic past. And the irony consists precisely in the reversal of the
view that the duncead had intended to convey, a reversal Pope is
careful to suggest over and over in the notes explaining his use
of the word 'Saturnian'. Thus he warns the reader that, though
'the ancient Golden Age is by Poets stiled *Saturnian*', still, 'in the
Chymical language, *Saturn* is Lead'.[1] The Saturnian age of the
Georges becomes, in the alchemy of the poem, an age of lumpish
dulness.

Such parodies as the above certainly constitute effective contemporary satire, yet a satire that it is impossible to confine to
the level of personal antipathy on Pope's part toward George II
or his laureate. It can be granted that Pope is using local, personal material; but it must be admitted at the same time that
such material becomes the bridge by which we cross to a land of
larger values. To say that Ambrose Philips was preferred for
wit under George II may be to express some personal feeling,
but it is also to strike at

> All who true dunces in her [Dulness'] cause appear'd,
> And all who knew those dunces to reward. (II 21–2)

It is to reveal an age characterized by a serious breakdown of
standards. How great the decline in standards the poem seeks to
express can be illustrated by the above lines. They are, after all,
a parody of these in the *Aeneid*, and serve to set the servants of
George—and Dulness—against the old heroic race found in
Virgil's Elysian fields:

> Here patriots live, who, for their country's good,
> In fighting fields, were prodigal of blood:
> Priests of unblemish'd lives here make abode,
> And poets worthy their inspiring god;
> And searching wits, of more mechanic parts,
> Who grac'd their age with new-invented arts:
> Those who to worth their bounty did extend,
> And those who knew that bounty to commend.
> (Dryden's trans., VI 895–902)

In applying the ancient resources to foolish purposes, the

1. *Twick. Ed.*, p. 63, note to l. 26.

dunces could reasonably be held to be corrupters of the classical structure of values. On the level of language this is easily grasped: after the Tates and Eusdens and Welsteds of an age have finished appropriating all its terms of value for their own irresponsible ends, those terms are no longer readily available for serious use; some of their meaning will have leaked away. Though Pope could refurbish and revitalize the resources of classical language in his own very self-conscious practice, it must have become more and more difficult to use this language of value in such a way that the full significance and worth of all that it comprehended would be conveyed.

And because the dunces were thus muddying up the inheritance flowing from Greece and Rome, it was again only fitting that they be exhibited at their unclean task in the *Dunciad*. No matter how mean and petty they might appear in that epic world, they were still to be shown as capable of befouling it. Hence the obscene parody of the ancient gymnastic ideal which occurs in Book II.

The scatological material in this episode serves as a symbol of the normal pursuits of dunces. As Pope points out,[1] there is a 'natural connection . . . between Libellers and common Nusances [*sic*]': the resemblance of one who deals in slander to a muddiver who flings mud 'and wide pollutes around' is easily enough realized. In a broader sense, too, the foul and degenerate activities serve as an imaginative manifestation of the debasement suffered by the classical ideal in the milieu of Dulness. Thus Virgil's portrayal of two heroic gauntlet fighters,

> One on his youth and pliant limbs relies;
> One on his sinews and his giant size,
> (Dryden's trans., v 570-1)

is twisted to serve in the *Dunciad* as a description of the urinary qualifications of Curll and Chetwood in their excretory exercise:

> This on his manly confidence relies,
> That on his vigor and superior size.   (II 161-2)

Maynard Mack has pointed out[2] that Pope builds up in the

1. Ibid., p. 107, note to l. 71.   2. *Pope and His Contemporaries*, p. 38.

Dunciad 'effects of striking epic richness, only to let them be broken down, disfigured, stained—as the word "vomit" stains the lovely movement and suggestion' of this line: 'And the fresh vomit run for ever green' (II 148). Pope's friend, Walter Harte, showed an awareness of the poet's procedure also; in the following lines he imitates Pope's parody[1] of Virgil's description of Magna Mater:

> When Rhet'ric glitters with too pompous pride,
> By this [parody], like *Circe*, 'tis un-deify'd.
> So *Berecynthia*, while her off-spring vye
> In homage to the Mother of the sky,
> (Deck'd in rich robes, of trees, and plants, and flow'rs,
> And crown'd illustrious with an hundred tow'rs)[2]
> O'er all *Parnassus* casts her eyes at once,
> And sees an hundred Sons—*and each a Dunce*.[3]

In Pope's verse, as in Harte's, the phrase 'and each a dunce' comes as a decided let-down; the hundred sons of Berecynthia were all gods. It is to this descent from epic richness of language that the word 'un-deify'd' refers in Harte's second line: the rhetoric, like the subject matter (the dunces), is un-deified. A simpler instance of this type of verbal plummeting occurs when Theobald, on his trip to the epic underworld of Book III, views the souls of dunces yet unborn:

> Millions and millions on these banks he views,
> Thick as the stars of night, or morning dews,
> As thick as bees o'er vernal blossoms fly,
> As thick as eggs at Ward in Pillory.   (23–6)

The glistening wave of epic similes[4] builds up until, at the last moment, it topples with a verbal crash.

So prolific is the *Dunciad* in examples of epic breakdown that one may well view the poem as a continual exemplification of

1. Cited above, p. 27.
2. Magna Mater was known as the 'turreted' goddess, and usually pictured as crowned with the towers of cities.
3. See p. 11 of Harte's *An Essay on Satire* as included in Richard Savage's *A Collection of Pieces in Verse and Prose . . . publish'd on Occasion of the DUNCIAD*. The critical value for the *Dunciad* of Harte's poem has not been fully appreciated.
4. Cf. *Aeneid*, VI 309 ff.; *Paradise Lost*, V 745–6.

the art of sinking in poetry. It is perhaps a question whether mock-epic poetry may not be defined as a very self-conscious exploitation of the qualities of bathos by an arrangement of the high alongside the low. If the art of sinking in poetry is largely a matter of permitting low and commonplace matter to follow in ludicrous contrast to the sublime, then Pope has more than proved his contention in Chapter IV of *Peri Bathous* 'that there is an art to the Bathos, or Profund'. Pope compels his verse to plummet downward, does wilful violence to its epic suggestions and movement; he accomplishes purposefully that which the dunces allowed to happen accidentally and unconsciously, and succeeds in imposing upon his victims precisely that bathetic quality he has accused them of possessing.

A good instance of more extended bathetic dramatization occurs at the moment when John Dennis is poised for his plunge into the muddy profound of the Thames:

> In naked majesty great Dennis stands,
> And, Milo-like, surveys his arms and hands,
> Then sighing, thus. "And I am now threescore?
> "Ah why, ye Gods! should two and two make four?"
> He said, and climb'd a stranded Lighter's height,
> Shot to the black abyss, and plung'd down-right.
> The Senior's judgment all the crowd admire,
> Who but to sink the deeper, rose the higher. (II 271–8)

Part of the passage, Pope points out in his notes,[1] is a parody of that 'verse of *Ovid*,

> —*Fletque Milon senior, cum spectat inanes*
> *Herculeis similes, fluidos pendere lacertos,*'[2]

and for an instant the parallel succeeds in investing the figure of Dennis with all the pathos the ruined might and grandeur of Milo call to mind. But the image is 'plung'd down-right' by the profound simplicity of mind exhibited by Dennis, and pathos is converted into bathos. The verses would appear to be an exam-

1. See *Twick. Ed.*, p. 135.
2. Here is Dryden's translation of the lines (*Metamorphoses*, XV 228–30):
> Now sapless on the verge of death he stands,
> Contemplating his former feet and hands;
> And Milo-like, his slacken'd sinews sees . . .

E

ple of the 'infantine' mode, where 'a Poet grows so very simple, as to think and talk like a child'.[1]

In the episode of the epic sacrifice the coincidence of epical and duncical contexts again aids in the creation of a bathetic situation. Theobald, about to offer his literary 'off-spring' to the flames, addresses them thus:

> Adieu my children! better thus expire
> Un-stall'd, unsold; thus glorious mount in fire
> Fair without spot; than greas'd by grocer's hands,
> Or shipp'd with Ward to ape and monkey lands,
> Or wafting ginger, round the streets to go,
> And visit alehouse where ye first did grow. (I 197–202)

Theobald's lament is a parody of the affecting words of Andromache in Book III of the *Aeneid*,[2] in the light of which his concern for the 'maiden sheets' of his books becomes especially absurd. In the imaginative 'double exposure' that parody creates one cannot regard the affliction of Theobald without awareness of the other, and really tragic, situation. What results is an awareness again of the distortion which the classical original must suffer if it is to be accommodated to duncery. As it enters the realm of dulness it is hardly possible for the purity of Andromache's pathos to be preserved.

However bathetic and lachrymose the dunces become (as in the last two examples), Pope still manages to disengage his own attitude from theirs, to keep his *poem* uncontaminated by its 'dull' subject matter. The poet has the problem of making dulness interesting, and also of illustrating the perversion of the classical world of values without himself appearing to be guilty of the perversion. A type of 'verbal distancing' occurs: between the emo-

1. *Peri Bathous*, Chap. XI.
2. Dryden translates the original thus:
> O only happy maid of Priam's race,
> Whom death deliver'd from the foes' embrace!
> Commanded on Achilles' tomb to die,
> Not forc'd, like us, to hard captivity,
> Or in a haughty master's arms to lie.
> In Grecian ships unhappy we were borne,
> Endur'd the victor's lust, sustain'd the scorn:
> Thus I submitted to the lawless pride
> Of Pyrrhus, more a handmaid than a bride ... (III 415–23)

tion of Theobald in the passage just above, for instance, and the attitude of the poet there intervene the romantic suggestions of 'ape and monkey lands', of the ginger being 'wafted' through the streets. The same technique of verbal distancing is particularly noticeable in Book II; there, in 'compliance to modern nicety', Pope claims that, in dealing with the obscene subject matter, he has 'remarkably enrich'd and colour'd his language, as well as rais'd the versification'.[1] This assertion has only annoyed some of his editors, Courthope protesting that 'so far is he from being entitled to any credit for refining his imagery by his art, that he only brings the nauseous nature of his materials into stronger relief by the beauty of the form under which he presents them'.[2] This is certainly true, and it is part of the satiric procedure, but Courthope overlooks the aloofness created by the beautiful verse. The alternately chaste, or mellifluous, or grand qualities of Pope's language enable him to keep his own hands clean no matter how much dung is tossed about.[3] With epic connotations and vigour he describes what on a strictly denotative level is no more than the arc followed by Curll's urine:

> Impetuous spread
> The stream, and smoking, flourish'd o'er his head
> So, (fam'd like thee for turbulence and horns,)
> Eridanus his humble fountain scorns,
> Thro' half the heav'ns he pours th' exalted urn;
> His rapid waters in their passage burn.[4]   (II 171–6)

With exotic softness he recounts Eusden's seduction by the 'nut-brown maids' of the city sewers:

> How young Lutetia, softer than the down,
> Nigrina black, and Merdamante brown,
> Vy'd for his love in jetty bow'rs below.[5]   (II 309–11)

---

1. See *Twick. Ed.*, pp. 106–7, note to l. 71. See also the statements by 'Martinus Scriblerus, of the Poem', p. 52.   2. EC, IV, p. 20.

3. Pope, following Addison, uses this image. See *Twick. Ed.*, p. 106, note to l. 71.

4. These verses appear to parody those in the *Aeneid* which describe the flaming passage of the arrow shot into the air by Acestes in the epic archery contest. See *Aeneid*, V 525 ff. For other sources, see *Twick. Ed.*, p. 122, note to l. 173.

5. Sutherland (*Twick. Ed.*, p. 139) explains the proper names: ' "Lutetia"

Walter Harte described Pope's procedure in this manner:
'Tho' Sense subsists', it is 'distinct from phrase or sound'.[1] Such
an explanation perhaps implies an unfortunate dichotomy between sense and ornament in writing. But it also constitutes
recognition, at least, of the method by which Pope stays at one
remove from his subject, and by which he hints that the dunces
—not the artist—are responsible for whatever befoulment is
going on.

The breakdown of language, the collapse of 'effects of striking
epic richness', which Pope causes so often to happen in the
Dunciad can be seen as the reflection, the linguistic emblem, of a
broader collapse in values the poet thought he observed in his
age. It is this more general collapse which Pope celebrates near
the end of Book III in the grand conclusion, the vision of the
Saturnian age of Dulness soon to be ushered in, a passage altered
in the *Dunciad* of 1729 so as to vibrate even more strongly than at
first with echoes of Virgil's Fourth Eclogue. Settle, recounting
to Theobald the nature of the coming event, exclaims:

> Proceed great days[2]! till Learning fly the shore,
> Till Birch shall blush with noble blood no more,
> Till Thames see Eton's sons for ever play,
> Till Westminster's whole year be holiday;
> Till Isis' Elders reel, their Pupils' sport;
> And Alma Mater lye dissolv'd in Port!
> Signs following signs lead on the Mighty Year;
> See! the dull stars roll round and re-appear.
>
> (III 329–36)

Dryden's translation best exhibits the connection between
Pope's verse and the poetic prophecy of Virgil:

> The last great age, foretold by sacred rhymes,
> Renews its finish'd course: Saturnian times

---

is the classical name for the modern Paris. The name was thought to be
derived from "its dirty situation". (*Grub-Street Journal*, April 17, 1735.
Lutum = clay, mud.)—"Merdamante" = filth-loving.'

1. See p. 11 of Harte's *An Essay on Satire* in Savage's *A Collection of Pieces in
Verse and Prose . . . publish'd on Occasion of the DUNCIAD*.

2. In a note to this phrase Pope directs the reader to its parallel in Eclogue
IV, l. 12.

> Roll round again; and mighty years, begun
> From their first orb, in radiant circles run.   (5-8)

In the new age of Dulness all the marks of civilization fade away:
dulness will spread, first over the polite world, then over all
England, until 'Learning fly the shore' and until 'Art after Art
goes out, and all is Night'. This of course amounts to a tremendous revolution in any civilized state of affairs. Even though the
Virgilian context, and the notion it gives of what a real Golden
Age would be like, stands as a scathing reproach to this dull
new world, still one must recognize that such a total alteration
of human conditions as that wrought by the sons of Dulness constitutes no mean accomplishment. That Pope did not wish the
power of duncery underestimated is apparent from his note to
Book III, l. 337:

> Do not gentle reader, rest too secure in thy contempt of the
> Instruments for such a revolution in learning, or despise such
> weak agents as have been described in our poem, but remem-
> ber what the *Dutch* stories somewhere relate, that a great part
> of their Provinces was once overflow'd, by a small opening
> made in one of their dykes by a single *Water-Rat*.

Here we are brought to the realization of one final point about
the *Dunciad*, one to which the poem's epic character contributes
substance: that is, no matter how despicable the individual
dunces appear, one must yet recognize that their achievements
—the establishment, with the help of their goddess, of a new
empire, the inauguration of a new age of Dulness in which traditional values are eradicated—are really and truly matters of
epic scope. In other words there comes a moment at which the
epic vehicle must be taken seriously, when a 'status of serious
menace' is given 'to all this ludicrous activity'.[1] There is something 'epic' about such a complete wrecking of civilization as the
poem assumes; an action of such magnitude deserves no poetic
associations less grand and 'heroic' than those provided by epic
poetry. However ill-fitting their heroic garb, one at last finds the
dunces invested with uncivilizing powers of epic proportions.

1. Maynard Mack, *Pope and His Contemporaries*, p. 38.

CHAPTER III

THE VARIORUM DUNCIAD

I

ON 28 June 1728, Pope wrote to Swift, saying:

> The Dunciad is going to be printed in all pomp. . . It will be
> attended with *Proeme, Prolegomena, Testimonia Scriptorum, Index
> Authorum*, and Notes *Variorum*. As to the latter, I desire you to
> read over the text, and make a few in any way you like best,
> whether dry raillery, upon the style and way of commenting
> of trivial critics; or humorous, upon the authors in the poem;
> or historical, of persons, places, times; or explanatory; or
> collecting the parallel passages of the ancients.[1]

The next year the transmogrified *Dunciad* appeared and, with
the addition of a huge and quite fanciful textual apparatus all
its own, exhibited a new and extremely complex dimension.
Most of the editorial paraphernalia is as much a construction of
the imagination as the poem, and, by virtue of the artistic dila-
tion which has occurred, one finds it possible to examine in a
better light certain abiding qualities of the satire.

That the quality of the new material attached to the poem has
never been adequately defined is due, I think, to the assumptions
most critics and editors have made: that the notes are to be taken
at the level of history, and that their main purpose is to continue
the personal satire in a prose commentary. The counter-assump-
tion that all this paraphernalia is a deliberate displacing of history, 'notes toward a supreme fiction', a consciously contrived
hoax (as Pope's own comment above suggests), has never been
widely entertained. Not, of course, a hoax in the sense of a cheap
trick; rather in the sense of a distortion of history so magnificent
and well-conceived that it has imposed upon the dunces a character Pope knew they never actually possessed (though many
readers have accepted it as 'truth'), and imposed upon editors

1. EC, VII, p. 134.

and critics a never-ending (though in part fruitless) job of clarification, a laborious correction of Pope's careful misstatements
of fact.

In this regard the *Dunciad* has shared the fate of another
Renaissance historical fiction, the hoax entitled *Epistolae Obscurorum Virorum*, which was executed in the early sixteenth century by a group of German humanists. The relationship between
the two works is, in fact, illuminating. Pope was familiar with
the *Epistolae* (a particularly elegant edition was published in
London in 1710 and dedicated to Steele[1]), and he was quite
aware of its affinity with his *Variorum*. At one point in the apparatus he remarks that 'letters sent us (tho' not to the purpose)
shall yet be printed under the title of *Epistolae Obscurorum
Virorum*; which, together with some others of the same kind
formerly laid by for that end, may make no unpleasant addition
to the future impressions of this poem'.[2] It has often been noted
that Steele never saw the irony of the *Epistolae*. Nor was he the
first to be deceived. Long ago Sir Thomas More had written to
Erasmus:

> It does one's heart good to see how delighted everybody is with
> the *Epistolae Obscurorum Virorum*. The learned are tickled by
> their humour, while the unlearned deem their teachings of
> serious worth. When we laugh, they think we do but deride
> the style; this they do not defend, but they declare that all
> faults are compensated by the weight of the matter... I verily
> believe that in a hundred years the dolts would not perceive
> the nose turned up at them—though larger than the snout of
> the rhinoceros![3]

In the *Epistolae* scholarly dolts who are foes to humanistic
learning are made to expose their folly in what purport to be

1. An account by Steele of the work is found in *Tatler*, no. 197, Thursday,
13 July 1710.
2. See the 'Advertisement to the First Edition, separate, of The Fourth
Book of the DUNCIAD', *Twick. Ed.*, pp. 410–11.
In a letter to John Caryll Pope speaks of John Reuchlin, until recent times
associated with the authorship of the *Epistolae*, as having tried to laugh certain monks of the middle ages out of the 'depths of barbarism' into which
they fell. See EC, VI, p. 148, n. 2.
3. Quoted by F. G. Stokes in the introduction to his edition of the
Epistolae Obscurorum Virorum (London, Chatto & Windus, 1909), p. xlix.

real letters addressed to a historical personage. Both the *Epistolae* and the *Dunciad* are embedded in a historical situation from which they do not seek to depart; they rather manipulate history by subjecting it to subtle violation. The integrity, the actuality, of plain matter of fact is steadily and relentlessly disregarded, and the writers proceed, by artful insinuations, slight but skilful prevarications, misquoting and misrepresenting, to the creation of a revised, a reformed history. The result of this fretting and corrosion of fact by fancy is a curiously ambiguous realm of half-truth in which the reader wanders, never quite sure as to the validity of what he reads, never certain what is fact, what is make-believe.

In both works one can accept this fictional situation the author has brought into existence, see that the whole creation lies somewhere in a twilight zone, and attempt to appreciate the whimsical tension between the real and the unreal the artist has fabricated; or else, dashing through thin and thick 'On German Crouzaz and Dutch Burgersdyck', one can set out determined to do justice to the hapless creatures so sorely maligned and mistreated by an irresponsible satirist. The latter approach has most often been that of the critics and editors of Pope. According to Lounsbury, for instance, Pope's prose commentary is mainly a 'fertile breeding-ground of baseless insinuation and deliberate misstatement',[1] which it is the duty of every right-thinking critic to repudiate. What such critics resolve to disregard is the fact that all art involves a distortion of the historical, the 'real'. It is only by imaginative alterations that St Joan or Henry V or Thomas à Becket enter the realm of art. Pope's 'baseless' manipulation of history, his 'vicious' misrepresentation of the dunces' real characters, is not only a part of the joke's effectiveness in giving discomfort to the dunces (and hence undoubtedly related to personal motives), but it is also a necessary part of the 'distancing' of the ephemeral in art, of getting the bee into the amber. Very few of the dunces were as interesting in real life as they are after Pope has retouched and given a lustre to their dulness.

1. *The Text of Shakespeare*, p. xiii. Lounsbury's statement is correct, but he obviously misses the ironic element involved in what he has discovered.

From the beginning of course the question of personality has played over and obscured the real nature of Pope's fiction, both in the poem and as it is developed in the notes. When the poet set out to scourge and damn to fame all who seemed bent on dismantling the humanist structure of values, he certainly did not hesitate to settle, at the same time, many personal scores. And whether the impetus to some of the satire was a matter of personal enmity or the 'strong antipathy of good to bad' (particularly of a good writer to bad writing), it was hardly to be expected that the *Dunciad* would arouse anything but the greatest sense of outrage in the dunces. For a period of fifteen years the atmosphere was filled with charge, protest, and countercharge. The spume of contemporary personality was inevitable; it was scarcely possible for the dunces to take an objective view of their injuries.

Since the day of Pope and the dunces, other forces have prolonged and exaggerated the emphasis on personality. One of these has been the romantic assumption about literature which has held sway during most of the two hundred years since Pope's death. Sound enough for its own purpose, the romantic assumption may not take us far with satire. For if all poetry is the result of the spontaneous overflow of powerful emotions, then one must decide that the emotions of satirists are invariably venomous, and conclude with Oliver Elton that the *Dunciad* is 'more seriously flawed than any other' poem that Pope wrote and that 'in criticizing it we had best be silent about his "art"'.[1] Indeed, if all poetry must be viewed as direct spiritual autobiography, then the *Dunciad* becomes the record of a personal feud which 'has no determinable significance beyond that',[2] and instead of talking of its 'poetic intensity extraordinarily rich in beauty, oddness and surprise',[3] we must talk of its 'tone of furious indiscriminate hatred, the half-crazed misanthropy of the whole poem . . .'[4]

1. *The Augustan Ages*, vol. VIII of the Periods of European Literature Series (Edinburgh and London, William Blackwood & Sons, 1899), p. 306.
2. See Henry W. Boynton's introduction to the Cambridge Edition of *The Complete Poetical Works of Pope* (Boston and New York, Houghton Mifflin Company, 1931), p. xvii.
3. See F. R. Leavis, *Revaluation* (New York, George W. Stewart, Inc., 1947), p. 89.
4. This is one of Gilbert Highet's reactions, *M.L.R.*, 36, p. 334.

The more one reads the *Dunciad* with an eye to history, the more one is likely to become inspired, by the poetic injustice of it all, to try to set the record straight. But more than half of the personages who appear in the poem were not even contemporary with Pope;[1] names were constantly being dropped from the text and others substituted; the sheer number of proper names (real names, English pseudonyms, classical nicknames, and cryptic initials) tends strongly toward individual anonymity. Pope himself maintained that his 'Poem was not made for' the dunces, but the duncas 'for the Poem'.[2] A too rigorous historical approach (and the personal concern for the victim it stimulates) is almost bound to assert the very kind of particularity the poem attempts to transcend.

These later intellectual obstructions to a proper understanding of the poem and of the expanded fiction of the *Variorum* apparatus have raised what amount to physical obstacles too—for every editor since Pope's time has heaped successive layers of apparatus and commentary upon the original, fanciful, apparatus. Thus it has become extremely difficult for a reader to disentangle Pope's fiction from the later editorial facts, to see his imaginative gloss undisturbed by corrections and additions which only succeed in turning his feigned history into true—but lifeless—history. If the results had not been so unfortunate, it would be entertaining to observe every editor carefully disassembling the poem's wholeness as a work of art into the discrete historical particulars from which Pope fashioned it.

The simple fact is that historical truth is distorted by Pope so as to be more metaphorical; with a large residue of actual duncery still clinging about them, he alters the personages of his poem to make them appear more perfect vehicles for his subject —dulness in human kind. At the same time, one is always conscious of the fact that the dunces *were* real people. But where the reality leaves off and the fancy begins is difficult for the reader to discover; we are faced with dunces who are neither wholly here—in the poem—nor there—in history.

1. Mr Highet states that in 'the first book of the *Dunciad* with 330 lines, there are thirty-six names of contemporaries and eighty-nine names altogether'. See *M.L.R.*, 36, p. 340.
2. See *Twick. Ed.*, p. 205.

Even before the reader approaches the expanded fiction in the notes, Pope has prepared him, through his manipulation of proper names in the poem, for the interplay of fact and fancy he is to encounter. In the smaller compass of a single word one can often see the tension between the real and the 'unreal' brought to a fine point, for the poem is full of names which not only refer to historical personages but also have an aura of imaginative meaning. Take for instance the following cacophonic passage (exemplifying the anarchic discord of dulness) in which the proper names are almost, but not quite, drowned:

> Now thousand tongues are heard in one loud din:
> The Monkey-mimicks rush discordant in.
> 'Twas chatt'ring, grinning, mouthing, jabb'ring all,
> And Noise, and Norton, Brangling, and Breval,
> Dennis and Dissonance; and captious Art,
> And Snip-snap short, and Interruption smart.
>
> (II 227–32)[1]

The proper names 'tend to take on a metaphorical colouring',[2] to lose some of their strictly personal quality. And though in this passage they largely retain their character as proper names, there are other instances in which they assume something like the full status of common nouns.

> Yes, to my Country I my pen consign,
> Yes, from this moment, mighty Mist! am thine.
>
> (I 193–4)

Even though Pope points out, in a note to these lines, that Nathaniel Mist was the publisher of a Tory newspaper, the reader's first response is likely to be an identification of the 'mighty Mist' with the goddess Dulness, who throughout the poem is associated with mist, clouds, and fog. Confronted with

1. All line references in this chapter, unless otherwise noted, are to the A text of the *Twick. Ed.*

2. See Maynard Mack, in *Pope and His Contemporaries*, p. 27. It should be noted that my discussion here is not about the metaphoric effects as such that Pope achieves by his use of names. That matter has already been treated by Mr Mack in the work cited here, and by W. K. Wimsatt in his essay 'Rhetoric and Poems: The Example of Pope', in *English Institute Essays, 1948* (New York, Columbia University Press, 1949), pp. 201–2. My discussion is concerned with showing how the names accord with the conjunction of the real and the imaginary found in Pope's historical fiction.

two possible interpretations, the reader wavers; a momentary
state of indecision is induced. Ideally, this is the state in which
he should remain; ideally, because to plump toward either the
strictly historical entity or the strictly fictional one is to destroy
the delicate and ambiguous perplexity into which Pope has
manœuvred him. As the names of the dunces move toward
another realm of reference their historical solidity appears com-
promised.[1]

In other examples Pope appears to be actually *creating* a new
meaning for a proper name. Consider for instance the problem
raised by the mysterious bird of Dulness which descends upon
Theobald's head:

> a monster of a fowl,
> Something betwixt a Heideggre and owl. (1 289–90)[2]

John James Heidegger in real life was manager of the opera
house at Haymarket, but here his name has been made to rever-
berate, wittily, with the rumour of 'all monstrous, all prodigious
things . . . Gorgons and Hydras, and Chimeras dire'. Never
again, inside the poem, can the name refer solely and strictly to
the historical Heidegger.

In the case of Theobald, this process of redefinition proves
still more significant, and with this example we return from the
poetic text to our main theme in this chapter, the historical fiction as developed in the *Variorum* notes. Pope, it should be noted,
almost invariably uses the disrespectful spelling 'Tibbald'
throughout the *Dunciad* and its fictional apparatus.[3] But the

---

1. Here is another example of this kind of ambiguity:
> High on a gorgeous seat, that far outshone
> Henley's gilt Tub, or Fleckno's Irish Throne,
> Or that, where on her Curlls the Public pours
> All-bounteous, fragrant grains, and golden show'rs . . . (11 1–4)
This is really a description of Edmund Curll in the stocks. But 'Curlls' suggests ringlets of hair as well, in which case the 'fragrant grains' refer, as
Sutherland points out (*Twick. Ed.*, p. 97, note to l. 4), to the refuse malt
thrown at Curll's head, or (as the word 'grain' did in the period) to a type
of dye.

2. I quote from the B text of the *Twick. Ed.* since there the name is spelled
out.

3. Mr Sutherland suggests (*Twick. Ed.*, p. 75, note to l. 106) that Theobald's name was given a trisyllabic pronunciation in Pope's time, but the evidence offered seems inconclusive. Perhaps two pronunciations were current.

important thing is that a 'Tibbald' has never been defined, and because of this the word tends to attract to itself, to pull in, any suggestive meanings the poet may place in its vicinity (just as occurs in the case of the word 'Heidegger'). By carefully controlling the context the poet can make the name become a name of whatever he chooses.[1] These lines by David Mallet which Pope quotes in his notes illustrate the point:

> With eye still earnest, and with bill declin'd,
> He picks up what his Patron drops behind;
> With such choice cates his palate to regale,
> And is the careful Tibbald of a Whale.[2]

The milieu of the word serves to give it its definition.

There is, even today, a tendency to look upon names as somehow defining personality, and in Pope's time this tendency still had the status of a self-conscious theory, originating in classical doctrines of etymological meaning such as are expounded in Plato's *Cratylus* and in the tradition of biblical interpretation that Adam, in naming the beasts that passed before him, had somehow, by virtue of his infused knowledge, defined their essence in the name given them.[3] The label names of a Plautus or

1. Another good example of Pope's technique is given by W. K. Wimsatt (*English Institute Essays, 1948*, pp. 201–2): 'Why is a certain scholar a graceless figure? Because his name shows it.

> Yet ne'er one sprig of laurel graced these ribalds,
> From slashing *Bentley* down to pidling *Tibbalds*.

Here the words *sprig* and *pidling* play a part too in proving what it means to have a name like that.'

The lines cited are from 'Epistle to Dr. Arbuthnot', 163–4.

2. See *Twick. Ed.*, p. 83, note to l. 164.

3. Denham opens 'The Progress of Learning' by referring to the tradition; it crops up in Donne's 'Satyre IIII', 'versified' by Pope thus:

> Scarce was I enter'd, when, behold! there came
> A thing which Adam had been posed to name.   (24–5)

A passage from a sermon by Robert South, whose works were widely known in the age, indicates the nature of the theory:

> [Adam] came into the world a philosopher, which sufficiently appeared by his writing the nature of things upon their names; he could view essences in themselves, and read forms without the comment of their respective properties.

See South's *Sermons Preached Upon Several Occasions* (Oxford, 1742), I, p. 31. Edward Lyford's *The True Interpretation and Etymologie of Christian Names* (London, 1655) contains an account of the idea in the preface to the reader.

a Ben Jonson or a Pope illustrate the tradition at the literary level. And of course the practice persists into recent times, with names such as Emily Brontë's *Heathcliff*, Trollope's *Proudie*, Eliot's *Prufrock*, *Gerontion*, and *Celia Coplestone*.

If one takes the view that names can somehow define personality, then to distort a person's name amounts to a distortion of his personality or identity. The Tibbald of the *Dunciad* is not quite the Theobald of history. Moreover the entire milieu of Pope's poem succeeds in suggesting that a Tibbald, something of which no one had ever heard before, is a species of dull writer, habitually maudlin and comatose. At the same time, the reader is still aware of the actual Theobald; there is a large residue of the historical person in the new entity. Pope does not wish the separation from history to be complete, for his notes constantly affirm that such a person really lived and wrote in 1728. The reader is once more faced with a problem in literary schizophrenia: should he read the poem in terms of Tibbald or of Theobald? Ideally, again, it would seem that he is to do both. The teasing ambivalence of the situation would be lost if either the historical Theobald or the imaginary Tibbald were to be pursued to the exclusion of the other. There is no doubt that Pope wished to eat his cake and have it too; he desired to satirize the historical Theobald while simultaneously amusing the reader with a Tibbald. For us to remove the dunces from this limbo, this 'neither' region, and place them in a heaven or hell of our own making, is to miss the point. The dunces should not escape their predicament, the realm of half-truth assigned them by Pope in these lines:

> Lo Bond and Foxton, ev'ry nameless name,
> All crowd, who foremost shall be damn'd to Fame.
>
> (III 151–2)

II

In the strange in-between world of the *Variorum* there is no more deliberate displacing of history than that contrived by the closest reader of all Pope's editors, Martinus Scriblerus. His procedures often imperil the very actuality of the dunces. The following lines are part of the scene in which Dulness creates a phantom poet as a prize for the booksellers:

> A Fool, so just a copy of a Wit;
> So like, that criticks said and courtiers swore,
> A wit it was, and call'd the phantom, More. (II 44–6)

The fantastic annotation to this passage starts off with a long and loosely accurate account of Pope's relations with James Moore-Smyth, concluding in this manner: 'Notwithstanding what is here collected of the Person imagin'd by *Curl* to be meant in this place, we cannot be of that opinion . . . since the name itself is not spell'd *Moore* but *More*; and lastly, since the learned *Scriblerus* has so well prov'd the contrary.' Then occurs the note containing the 'proof' of Scriblerus that the person suggested by the name 'More' (obviously Moore-Smyth) had no actual existence:

> It appears . . . that this is not the name of a real person, but fictitious; *More* from μωρός, *stultus*, μωρία, *stultitia*, to represent the folly of a Plagiary.

The above note is only one of several which operate to deprive the duces of historical integrity, to put their existence in jeopardy, or at least to deny and minimize it to the extent that it becomes less contemporary, less determinately historical, less 'real'. This de-historizing pressure is continuous. The duces become more and more 'obscure men'. In the following lines Dulness sponsors a second race for phantom personalities:

> Three wicked imps of her own Grubstreet Choir
> She deck'd like Congreve, Addison, and Prior;
> Mears, Warner, Wilkins run: Delusive thought!
> Breval, Besaleel, Bond, the Varlets caught.
>
> (II 115–18)

Here Scriblerus puts in:

> I foresee it will be objected from this line, that we were in an error in our assertion on verse 46. of this Book, that *More* was a fictitious name, since these persons are equally represented by the Poet as phantoms. So at first sight it may seem; but be not deceived, Reader! these also are not real persons. 'Tis

true *Curl* declares *Breval* a Captain, author of a Libel call'd *The Confederates*: But the same *Curl* first said it was written by *Joseph Gay*:[1] Is his second assertion to be credited any more than his first? He likewise affirms *Bond* to be one who writ a Satire on our Poet; but where is such a Satire to be found? where was such a Writer ever heard of? As for *Besaleel*, it carries Forgery in the very name, nor is it, as the others are, a surname.[2] Thou may'st depend on it no such authors ever liv'd: All phantoms!

To dismiss, as Pope does, certain dunces with the statement 'These were people who writ about the year 1726'; to comment on a person who 'wrote numbers of books which are not come to our knowledge'; to advise the reader to see 'Eusden's *whole Works* (*if to be found*)'[3]—all this is not merely an acute annoyance to the victim, and a source of humour to the reader; it amounts finally to a serious impairment of the victim's historical status. In his comment on these lines,

> True to the bottom, see Concanen creep,
> A cold, long-winded, native of the deep, (II 287–8)

Pope notes:

> In the former editions there were only Asterisks in this place; this name [Concanen] was since inserted merely to fill up the verse, and give ease to the ear of the reader.

One thinks of the Astrologer Partridge, 'buried alive' and 'dead' under the fictional circumstances imposed upon his existence by Swift and his circle, another instance of comic tension between the real and the unreal. Writers like Morrice, Curll, Dennis, all those spectres and shadows whose names flit through the scenes of the poem, appear deprived of the very solidity and identity which the notes, in another sense, insist that they possess. Just as one knows that those who people Dante's *Inferno* are 'real' persons who have somehow been translated to

1. A really fictitious name used by Curll to mislead readers into thinking that works under the name of J. or Joseph Gay were by John Gay. Cf. Pope's note to II 120.
2. The writer's name was Bezaleel Morrice.
3. See I, note to l. 168; II, note to l. 199; I, note to l. 71.

a sphere of the timeless, so Pope has placed the dunces in a type of purgatory—a comic one.

> Next plung'd a feeble, but a desp'rate pack,
> With each a sickly brother at his back:
> Sons of a Day! just buoyant on the flood,
> Then number'd with the puppies in the mud.
> Ask ye their names? I could as soon disclose
> The names of these blind puppies as of those.
> Fast by, like Niobe (her children gone)
> Sits Mother Osborne,[1] stupify'd to stone!
> And Monumental Brass this record bears,
> "These are,—ah no! these were, the Gazetteers!"[2]

Scriblerus in a note to these lines confidently asserts that

We ought not to suppress that a modern Critic here taxeth the Poet with an Anachronism, affirming these Gazetteers not to have lived within the time of his poem, and challenging us to produce any such paper of that date. But we may with equal assurance assert, these Gazetteers not to have lived since, and challenge all the learned world to produce one such paper at this day. Surely therefore, where the point is so obscure, our author ought not to be censured too rashly.

As the dunces, subjected to Pope's fancy, become less and less 'real', the poet proceeds to give them increasing amounts of quite non-historical personality. Proceeding with unembarrassed ease through misrepresentation and misquotation Pope 'essentializes' for the reader perfect dunces—in whom, however, the clay of the historical original is still to be seen. And it is just where the factual or historical semblance is most pronounced that one finds the policy of misstatement most patiently and thoroughly pursued. One of the most frequent methods is to make the dunces seem to deny something that has not even been charged and thus raise the question of a guilt in themselves or their friends which the poet, presumably, has not even been aware of. This is part of the prevailing technique of self-exposure

1. Osborne was the pseudonym for James Pitt. See *Twick. Ed.*, p. 311, note to l. 312.
2. These lines, and the accompanying notes, are to be found in the B Text of the *Twick. Ed.*, pp. 310–11.

F

found in both the *Epistolae Obscurorum Virorum*[1] and the *Dunciad*.
No one suffers more, in this respect, than John Dennis, who
makes his appearance in the notes a greater number of times
than anyone else, and whom Pope is constantly damning out of
his own mouth. One of the most hilarious instances occurs in the
note to these lines:

> Behold yon pair, in strict embraces join'd;
> How like their manners, and how like their mind!
> Fam'd for good-nature, B[urnet] and for truth;
> D[uckett] for pious passion to the youth.   (III 173–6)

After assuring the reader that these lines are merely a literal
translation of Virgil (*Aeneid*, v 293–6) and surely 'never interpreted in a perverse sense', the note goes on:

> But it will astonish the Reader to hear, that on no other occa-
> sion than this line, a Dedication was written to this Gentle-
> man [Duckett] to induce him to think something farther.
> "Sir, you are known to have all that affection for the beautiful
> part of the creation which God and Nature design'd.—Sir,
> you have a very fine Lady—and, Sir, you have eight very fine
> Children,"—*&c.* [*Dedic. to* Dennis *Rem. on the Rape of the
> Lock.*][2] The truth is, the poor Dedicator's brain was turn'd
> upon this article; he had taken into his head that ever since
> some *Books* were written against the *Stage*, and since the
> *Italian Opera* had prevail'd, the nation was infected with a vice
> not fit to be nam'd. He went so far as to print upon this sub-
> ject, and concludes his argument with this remark, "that he
> cannot help thinking the Obscenity of Plays excusable at this
> juncture, since, when that execrable sin is spread so wide, it
> may be of use to the reducing men's minds to the natural
> desire of women." Dennis, *Stage defended* against Mr. *Law*,
> p. 20. Our author has solemnly declared to me, he never
> heard any creature but the Dedicator mention that Vice and
> this Gentleman together.

Dennis's officious and damaging defence of 'this Gentleman',

---

1. See Stokes's introduction to the *Epistolae Obscurorum Virorum*, pp. xlv–xlvi.
2. Pope's brackets. Dennis's *Remarks on the Rape of the Lock* appeared after
the publication of the *Dunciad*. See E. N. Hooker, *The Critical Works of John
Dennis* (Baltimore, The Johns Hopkins Press, 1939, 1943), II, p. 512.

his parade of the 'very fine Lady' and the 'eight very fine Children' as proof of sexual normality, his support of stage obscenity as a safeguard against homosexuality (there is an air of the ingenious 'projector' in this), all these elements make him appear, in the note, too preposterous to be 'real'—a fantastic. Yet Pope did not make the whole thing up; it was a matter of stretching the facts ever so slightly here and there.

Besides Dennis, any number of other dunces are caught up in Pope's web of fantasy. Here is Pope's digest of an account written by Henley of himself:[1]

> He [Henley] had the *assurance* to form a Plan which no mortal ever thought of; he had success against all opposition; challenged his adversaries to fair disputations, and *none would dispute with him*; writ, read and studied twelve hours a day; compos'd three dissertations a week on all subjects; undertook to teach in *one year* what Schools and Universities teach in *five*; was not terrify'd by menaces, insults or satyrs, but still proceeded, matured his bold scheme, and put the *Church* and *all that*, in *danger*.

Sutherland comments that this passage, lifted from Henley's *Oratory Transactions*, *No. 1*, represents 'Pope's usual paraphrase'.[2] It does indeed. Henley was generally considered a quack and charlatan, but this note makes him a 'character'. It is not a question of what Henley really said, but what a dunce might say. Henley's duncery is 'perfected'.[3]

Thus, by a slight change of emphasis achieved by italicization,

1. Ostensibly the account of Henley quoted by Pope was written by a certain 'Welstede', obviously meant to pass as Leonard Welsted. Pope hints the account is by Henley himself, and Sutherland agrees. See *Twick. Ed.*, pp. 173–4, note to l. 195.

2. *Twick. Ed.*, p. 174.

3. As is that of Theobald, when it is said of him that

He writ a Poem call'd the *Cave of Poverty*, which concludes with a very extraordinary Wish, 'That some great Genius, or man of distinguished merit may be *starved*, in order to celebrate her [Poverty's] power, and describe her Cave.' It was printed in octavo, 1715.

Theobald's poem was printed in 1714, and, as Sutherland points out (note to l. 226, p. 90, *Twick. Ed.*), the words 'are not, as might be supposed, Theobald's. Pope is paraphrasing—and in doing so travesties—stanza cxx of Theobald's poem'. But he has also made Theobald appear a little more simple-minded than he really was, has made him into a 'Tibbald'.

or the shifting of punctuation, or the studied misquoting of history and biography, the dunces are made to expose that *gravity* of mind and those *extraordinary* traits of character they possess, and to enter the semi-historical limbo of the poem. An example which will sum up the whole procedure is the note in which the following passage occurs:

> Mr. *Dennis* is *excellent* at pindarick writings, *perfectly regular* in all his performances, and a person of *sound Learning*.

We are told that the information is derived from an account written by 'Dennis *of himself*', and we are referred to '*Jacob*'s Lives of Dram. Poets, page 68. 69. *compared with* page 286'.[1] Pp. 68 and 69, about Dennis, were actually written by Jacob, but are misinterpreted by Pope in the light of p. 286, where Jacob alludes to the autobiographical information he has received from Dennis and others. Dennis went to the point of publishing a letter from Jacob denying the charge. (Such was the expostulation and reply aroused among the dunces and the magnitude of the 'history' Pope 'arranged'.) Then Pope inserted the denials and protestations of innocence made against such charges by Dennis and other dunces (with, again, some slight alteration) in the apparatus of later editions of the poem.[2]

Throughout the *Variorum* one wanders in a gallery of retouched portraits. There is the bland stare of James Ralph who, on

> Being advised to read the Rules of Dramatick Poetry before he began a Play . . . smil'd and reply'd, *Shakespear writ without Rules*;[3]

the confident precocity of

> Mrs. *Susanna Centlivre*, wife to Mr. *Centlivre*, Yeoman of the Mouth to his Majesty. She writ many Plays, and a song . . . before she was seven years old. She also writ a Ballad against Mr. *Pope*'s *Homer* before he begun it;[4]

1. Note to I 104. See p. 74 of *Twick. Ed.*
2. See *Twick. Ed.*, p. 197, 'Errata. M. Scriblerus Lectori', and note by Sutherland.
3. See note to III 159.   4. See note to II 379.

the 'tremendous' scowl of John Dennis (having devised a new means of producing stage thunder) when

> at a Tragedy of a new Author with a friend of his, he fell into a great passion at hearing some [thunder], and cry'd "S'death! that is *my* Thunder."[1]

As in the *Epistolae Obscurorum Virorum*, where it is occasionally suggested that Johann Pfefferkorn's wife is very accommodating to the obscure men or that Magister Ortwin Gratius is the bastard son of a priest, so in the *Dunciad* there are those instances where it is hinted that Chetwood is uxorious, that Curll has a venereal 'condition', or that, as we have seen, Duckett is homosexual. It seems impossible to discover whether some of these statements are historically accurate;[2] they may well represent the same malformation of personality, the same wresting of actuality, so obvious throughout the notes at large. In the absence of proof one may contend that this, along with all the other distortions, constitutes libel of the worst sort. At the same time, however, it must be remembered that some kind of distortion is always an artistic necessity. As the epic hero is 'distanced' by the epic convention—must have certain physical and moral virtues, engage in certain exalted enterprises, 'live' on a higher plane of existence—so the dunces are 'distanced', projected into the realm of art, by a contrary convention. If the epic hero has certain expected attributes, so has the dunce: his morals will not be of the best, his sensitivity not of the finest, his enterprises questionable. Ordinary mortality is heightened and exalted in the one convention, elevating Elizabeth to Gloriana; it is lowered and debased in the other, depressing Theobald into Tibbald.

The dunces endure a type of historical death and imaginative transfiguration. This has been described best, perhaps, by Pope himself. When Theobald meets Settle, his 'father Anchises', on the visit to the underworld of Book III, the latter is described as appearing 'old in new state, another yet the same'. In the presence of such entities both real and unreal, the reader himself is asked to participate in a mixed awareness. It is always a case of

1. See note to II 218.
2. See note to II 175, and comment by Sutherland, *Twick. Ed.*, p. 123.

both/and, never a simple either/or. For anyone who cannot suffer such a state of affairs, the simplest solution is either to see the persons involved as types, the situation as wholly fictional-ized, or on the other hand, to read the notes primarily from the point of view of personal satire, to insist that the satire cannot be understood unless we know a great deal about the people con-cerned, to see the poem as a historical document. Actually, neither of these attitudes in isolation is supported by the poem, which simultaneously affirms and denies its historical connec-tions at every moment. The delicate and ridiculous equilibrium between fact and fancy that Pope has poised is immediately knocked out of balance by a one-sided approach. And though this perplexing and comic interchange of position, this syn-chronous negation and affirmation of their reality must have been very disturbing to the dunces personally, it is, after all, the best possible expression of the relationship between nonentity and being, bad art and good art, annihilation and creation, which Pope (as we shall see) has made the philosophic heart of his poem.

III

The notes added to the poem in 1729 are a concession by Pope that his original poetic text is flawed in one important respect. For what the notes often do is provide us with the justification for many of the satiric thrusts in the poem. In the new apparatus Pope frequently presents us with a bill of particulars which illu-minates and justifies indictment of particular dunces in the poem. Often in the poem itself an individual is damned without an immediate dramatization of his particular folly. Individuals are frequently *called* dunces, but not always in the poem are they *shown to be* dunces. This particular characteristic of the original three-book version of the poem is in marked contrast to the situ-ation in Book IV, for in this latter book Pope creates dunces, usu-ally anonymous, who immediately reveal their duncery in action and speech. Pope carefully included in the poetic text of Book IV the kind of justification for his satire which earlier he had had to supply by textual annotations.

The artistic failure to justify dramatically much of the original satire accounts for the occasionally abusive tone of the original three books, and explains, partly at least, the objections so many critics have raised against the poem. Because the poem is a satire (and therefore concerned with the creation of a combined artistic and ethical perspective), this failure was bound to suggest certain shortcomings in Pope's moral vision. It was bound to suggest (as was undoubtedly true on occasion) that Pope personally was not concerned with the justice of his attacks on individuals whom he calls dunces, and cared little in the poem to do more than damn his enemies out of hand.

The notes, then, are an implicit admission of a kind of failure, but they are also an attempt to remedy the situation, particularly with regard to the ethical vision of the poet. Because the notes are not the poem, however, even the remedy is not ultimately a thoroughly satisfactory solution to the problem: the damage is in some ways skilfully repaired, but one can still see the patches. Pope refused to attempt the kind of integrative process he undertook when he incorporated the epic machinery into *The Rape of the Lock*; he attempts instead merely to shore up the earlier structure of his poem.

One of the most important functions of the notes, therefore, is the creation of a new perspective on the characters and activities of the dunces. In the poem they are often made to appear little more than an antic crowd of Yahoos (as in the epic exercises), almost sub-human in their mud-diving, their cat-calling, their urinating. But many of the notes, and especially some of those written by Scriblerus, begin to rescue the dunces from the sub-human status in which the poem appeared to place them and to show them engaged in more realistic human folly. The tendency of the notes is often paradoxical: the satire against the dunces is sharpened or given more 'point' by the commentary, but at the same time, because the dunces are seen more and more as participating in the ordinary human 'condition' (and less and less as mere burlesque symbols), the satire is broadened in scope and the quality of mere abuse is diminished. The ordinary human condition is one of suffering and weakness which we can all not only understand but to some extent sympathize with.

The way in which the notes demand that the reader take a

new attitude toward the dunces can be indicated by the comment which accompanies Theobald's sacrifice of his works. Here Theobald addresses his literary offspring:

> Adieu my children! better thus expire
> Unstall'd, unsold; thus glorious mount in fire
> Fair without spot ...   (I 197–9)

Here is the note:

> This is a tender and passionate Apostrophe to his own Works which he is going to sacrifice, agreeable to the nature of man in great affliction, and reflecting like a parent, on the many miserable fates to which they would otherwise be subject.

Nothing could be more true. The note turns toward us, despite its satiric edge, a new aspect of the dunces, their participation in a kind of common human wretchedness. Having once considered Theobald as genuinely sharing in the sorrow any man might feel over the destruction of his work, it is henceforward impossible to dismiss the idea. A somewhat more sober comprehension of the events of duncery is offered to the reader.

The exegetical activities of Scriblerus are often comic treatments of potentially tragic material. Consider, for example, his commentary on the lines dedicated to Curll's urinary prowess.

> Thro' half the heav'ns he pours th' exalted urn;
> His rapid waters in their passage burn.   (II 175–6)

Scriblerus says:

> I am aware after all, that *burn* is the proper word to convey an idea of what was said to be Mr. *Curl*'s condition at that time. But from that very reason I infer the direct contrary. For surely every lover of our author will conclude he had more humanity, than to insult a man on such a misfortune or calamity, which could never befal him purely by his *own fault*, but from an unhappy communication with another.

Since the reader may conceivably not have noticed this significance in the word 'burn' before Scriblerus, in proof of his exegetical alertness, brings it into the open, his comment defeats his ostensible purpose of defending Pope against a charge of abusing

Curll. But in exposing Curll's 'condition' (and thereby sharpening the satire), Scriblerus also succeeds in placing it, however comically, firmly in the realm of evils the flesh is heir to. His statement that Curll's misfortune did not 'befal him purely by his own fault', while obtuse on his part, witty on Pope's, contains, as basis of both its obtuseness and its wit, the recognition that man is involved in imperfection, and suffers from it.

One of the most important notes in the *Variorum* is that which is appended to l. 41, Book i. After speaking of the '*Candour* and *Humanity* which everywhere appears' in the author towards those 'unhappy Objects of the Ridicule of all mankind, the bad Poets', the note goes on to say that the author

> imputes all scandalous rhimes, scurrilous weekly papers, lying news, base flatteries, wretched elegies, songs, and verses (even from those sung at Court, to ballads in the streets) not so much to Malice or Servility as to Dulness; and not so much to Dulness, as to Necessity; And thus at the very commencement of his Satyr, makes an Apology for all that are to be satyrized.

The note of course is part of an elaborate procedure exemplified frequently in the commentary by the application of such terms as 'humane' and 'humanity' to the 'author' himself and designed to establish a *persona*, that of a 'good man', for the poet. In suggesting that the acts of duncery are more the inevitable products of the human situation than they are the products of personal malice, Pope is conducting, however, an 'Apology' not only for himself but also for his victims. A depersonalized perspective, one which places the acts of duncery in a pattern of imperfection wider than that formed by Pope's personal enemies, is thereby created.

The creation in the notes of a kind of mock-charitable attitude on the part of the 'author' is in accord with the attempt to shift the dunces from mere Yahooism (and the satire from mere abusiveness) to a more recognizable human status. This mimic charity certainly permits Pope to give another turn to the screw, but at the same time it also alters the satiric balance. If we have not viewed with some faint feeling of fellowship, as well as with some laughter, Theobald's sacrifice of his poetic 'children', the

blanket awarded Curll, the sorrow of Dennis in his old age,[1] if
we have not eyed with a certain faint sympathy the poverty of
the dunces, then the notes occasionally serve, in ironic and
comic and incongruous fashion, to remind us of our own insensi-
tivity. This, for instance, is the note to the lines addressed by
Dulness to the mud-divers:

> A pig of lead to him who dives the best.
> A peck of coals a-piece shall glad the rest.   (II 269–70)

Pope remarks:

> Our indulgent Poet, whenever he has spoken of any dirty or
> low work, constantly puts us in mind of the Poverty of the
> offenders, as the only extenuation of such practices. Let any
> one but remark, when a Thief, a Pickpocket, a Highwayman
> or a Knight of the Post is spoken of, how much our hatred to
> those characters is lessen'd, if they add, a *needy* Thief, a *poor*
> Pickpocket, a *hungry* Highwayman, a *starving* Knight of the
> Post, &c.

Without the note one might see the 'peck of coals' as only another weight for sinking. The note makes it a symbol of the
dunces' poverty and hence a reminder that their activities are
not inspired only by 'Malice or Servility'. The comment further
embarrasses the position of the dunces, but it does so in terms
which also extenuate their deeds. A little later Scriblerus again
suggests (though again with irony) that the author entertains
some sympathy for the dunces:

> *Bavius* was an ancient Poet, celebrated by *Virgil* for the like
> cause as *Tibbald* by our author, tho' in less christian-like man-
> ner: For heathenishly it is declared by *Virgil* of *Bavius*, that he
> ought to be *hated* and *detested* for his evil works; *Qui Bavium non
> odit*—whereas we have often had occasion to observe our
> Poet's great good nature and mercifulness, thro' the whole
> course of this Poem.

The issue here is not of course Pope's personal and private attitudes towards the dunces as they were in real life.

Looming constantly between the reader and the text, expos-

---

1. See I 197–202, II 133–48, II 271–4.

ing himself and the 'author' as well as the dunces, yet at the same time introducing new and surprising motives and attitudes, the character of Scriblerus, in many different moods, is presented to the reader for appraisal: righteously indignant, tender-hearted, literal-minded, alternately acute and obtuse, and frequently much pleased with himself. Carrying a heavy satiric burden himself, Scriblerus yet engages our sympathy by virtue of his compassion for his fellow creatures, his generosity towards his professed enemies. These feelings reflect credit on himself at the same time that they guide the reader to a better vision of all the foolery.

A striking instance of the benevolent character of Scriblerus himself occurs in the notes to these lines describing a drunken poet lying in the street:

> How Laurus lay inspir'd beside a sink,
> And to mere mortals seem'd a Priest in drink.

(II 393–4)

Scriblerus comments:

This line presents us with an excellent Moral, that we are never to pass judgment merely by *appearances*; a Lesson to all men who may happen to see a reverend person in the like situation, not to determine too rashly, since not only the Poets frequently describe a Bard inspir'd in this posture,

> (*On* Cam's *fair bank where* Chaucer *lay inspir'd,*

and the like) but an eminent Casuist tells us, that if a Priest be seen in any indecent action, we ought to account it a deception of sight, or illusion of the Devil, who sometimes takes upon him the shape of Holy men on purpose to cause scandal. How little the prophane author of the *Characters of the Times* printed 8°. 1728. regarded this admonition, appears from these words pag. 26. (speaking of the reverend Mr. *Laurence Eusden*) "A most worthy successor of *Tate* in the Laureateship, a man of insuperable modesty, since certainly it was not his Ambition that led him to seek this illustrious post, but his affection to the Perquisite of *Sack*." A reflection as mean as it is scandalous!

'Laurus' in the above lines is the Latin word for 'laurel' and thus could easily designate the Laureate, 'Mr. Laurence Eusden'

(Laurence and Laurus are almost homonymic, too), whom Scriblerus defends so bravely. Thus the good scholiast is seen to attack someone else (Curll, presumably, for Pope believed him to be, as Sutherland notes, part-author of *The Characters of the Times*) for the very fault (gossip about priestly intemperance) which the poet he defends has also committed. Not only does he fail to comprehend what he is doing, but actually makes clear that Eusden is intended by 'Laurus'. His fumbling efforts to avoid scandal thus only serve to identify a victim and to direct Pope's satire toward a particular personality. But the *ad hominem* quality of the stroke at Eusden is at the same time caught up and finally even dissipated in the 'broader' humour of the note and our laughter at Scriblerus. Whether we are conscious of it or not, what Pope enables us to do is to laugh more innocently at the 'weakness' of Eusden; what may have been little more than a jeer at drunkenness passes into a healthier humour.

The comic and pathetic unawareness so typical of Scriblerus is qualified, however, by the keenness of some of his textual insights. Much of his textual technique, while obviously parodying that of Theobald and Bentley (it is a good anticipation of the latter's procedure in his edition of *Paradise Lost*), is more than justified by the light it sheds on elements in the poetic text likely to be overlooked by a casual reader.

> Wond'ring he gaz'd: When lo! a Sage appears,
> By his broad shoulders known, and length of ears.
>
> (III 27–8)

Scriblerus bungles into an exposition of the pun in this passage ('length of ears') as follows:

> This is a *sophisticated* reading. I think I may venture to affirm all the Copyists are mistaken here: I believe I may say the same of the Criticks; *Dennis, Oldmixon, Welsted*, have pass'd it in silence: I have always stumbled at it, and wonder'd how an error so manifest could escape such accurate persons...
>
> A very little Sagacity (which all these Gentlemen therefore wanted) will restore to us the true sense of the Poet, thus,
>
> By his broad shoulders known, and length of *years*.

See how easy a change! of one single letter! That Mr. *Settle* [the Sage] was old is most certain, but he was (happily) a stranger to the Pillory.

The point has been underlined for us by Mr Empson in the following remark—itself curiously Scriblerian: 'evidently this process is more valuable than Pope thought; the emendation would throw a great deal of light on his line, if any were needed, by insisting on the subdued pun which gives it its point, its innocent and colloquial ease'.[1]

The logic of the Scriblerian emendations would be perfectly valid if it were not for the fact that poetry, like life, is not susceptible of wholly logical analysis—that it is, to a great extent, alogical. Scriblerus's activities are a fine exhibition of a man floundering before a mystery. Here is a crux over which he exercises himself in the Specimen of his *Virgilius Restauratus*:

> apparent rari nantes in gurgite vasto,
> *arma virùm.*[2]

According to Scriblerus the correct reading is *Armi hominum*:

> Ridicule anteà *Arma virum* quae ex ferro conflata, quomodo possunt *natare*?

What amounts to an apparently non-logical expression, even perhaps a 'turn', in Virgil is submitted to a thoroughly straightforward kind of logic: the neuter, *arma* (arms in the sense of

1. William Empson, *Seven Types of Ambiguity* (New York, New Directions, 1947), p. 86.
An ancient rhetorical tradition lies behind the verbal effect Pope is practising in this example. Thus Aristotle: 'And what Theodorus calls "novel expressions" arise when what follows is paradoxical, and, as he puts it, not in accordance with our previous expectation; just as humorists make use of slight changes in words. The same effect is produced by jokes that turn on a change of letter; for they are deceptive. These novelties occur in poetry as well as in prose; for instance, the following verse does not finish as the hearer expected:

And he strode on, under his feet chilblains,

whereas the hearer thought he was going to say "sandals".' See *The 'Art' of Rhetoric*, trans. by J. H. Freese, The Loeb Classical Library (London, William Heinemann; New York, G. P. Putnam's Sons, 1926), pp. 409–11 (III xi 6).
2. *Aeneid*, I 118–19. This is Specimen VI of the *Virgilius Restauratus*, from which, since I suppose it is usually neglected by readers, I have taken this example instead of from the notes proper.

'weapons') gives way to the masculine *armus* (the limb of a man).
The reasoning is perfect (even hard to refute), but how inade-
quate and near-sighted! And as Scriblerus moves from one
such enigma to another, continually fumbling the real issue but
always pleased with himself, the comedy begins to merge into a
spectacle of the predicament of perfect rationality in a world it
never understands. The reader follows, laughingly, the mental
process of the eternally well-meaning critic, sees how he arrives
at the judgement he makes, and then, at the last moment, stands
amazed at the sight of a mind defeated in its aim of comprehension by trusting solely to its logical powers.

Editors and critics of Pope have long sought the origin of the
Dunciad in Dryden's *Mac Flecknoe*.[1] This view certainly has some
validity, but it overlooks a far wider satiric alliance in which the
Dunciad participates. The *Epistolae Obscurorum Virorum*, the *Praise
of Folly* of Erasmus, *Gulliver's Travels*, and the *Dunciad* all participate in a tradition which insists primarily upon an examination of man's condition and his ambiguous relationship to the
world about him. All are studies of mankind; all, in one way or
another, are ironic contemplations of man's general propensity
to folly. And the more one explores the increasing inclusiveness
of the *Dunciad* (through the addition of the notes and the Fourth
Book), the more one is aware of its implicit kinship with *An
Essay on Man*, of the latter's status as a more sober counterpart to
the ironic examination conducted in the *Dunciad*. As one of the
finest statements in English of the principles of Christian Socratism, *An Essay on Man* provides the best background against
which one may view the lack of self-knowledge which is so inseparable a part of Pope's characterization of Scriblerus and of
duncery in general.

Swift's Gulliver was never so wrong as when, at the end of his
travels, he put his whole trust in the complete and inhuman
rationalism of a Houyhnhnm point of view. From this too great
confidence in reason arose that pride, that 'reas'ning pride',
which Pope's *Dunciad* joins the work of Swift in repudiating.
What gave the greatest impetus to much of the satire written by
Pope and Swift was their awareness of the failure of the human

1. Cf. *Twick. Ed.*, p. xxxviii.

mind to realize that human reason is limited and fallible. This stimulated their attacks on school divines, deists, Cartesians, textual critics, and minute philosophers. Just as we see in Gulliver the fate of a man who relies too heavily on what appears most safe and stable—his own reason—so we can see in Scriblerus the pathetic figure of a being filled with pride in his own reason, and utterly unconscious that reason has betrayed him.

If the defects of Scriblerus are primarily intellectual failings, so are those of the dunces. More important, they are failings ultimately traceable to a lack of self-knowledge.[1] The theme of self-knowledge is announced with the utmost clarity in the letter to the publisher of the *Dunciad* signed by William Cleland (Pope's spokesman):

> There remains what in my opinion might seem a better plea for these people, than any they have made use of. If Obscurity or Poverty were to exempt a man from satyr, much more should Folly or Dulness, which are still more involuntary, nay as much so as personal deformity. But even this will not help them: Deformity becomes the object of ridicule when a man sets up for being handsome: and so must Dulness when he sets up for a Wit.[2]

Scriblerus himself points out that the poverty of the dunces results from the 'neglect of their proper talent thro' self conceit of greater abilities',[3] and Pope remarks in a note that the 'misfortune' of James Moore-Smyth 'was too inordinate a passion to be thought a Wit':

> Here is a very strong instance [the note goes on], attested by Mr. *Savage* son of the late Earl *Rivers*: who having shown some verses of his in manuscript to Mr. *Moore*, wherein Mr. *Pope* was call'd *first of the tuneful train*, Mr. *Moore* the next morning sent

1. For an example of Scriblerus' lack of self-knowledge, the logical corollary to his vain opinion of his own reasoning power, see the note to II 179 (*Twick. Ed.*, p. 123) where his wrathful indignation leads him to condemn, in others, the very exegetical methods he himself practises. A good parallel to this note, one that illustrates nicely the relation in which the dunces stand to Scriblerus, is that to II 134 (*Twick. Ed.*, p. 115). In this note John Dennis commits the very fault he inveighs against.

2. *Twick. Ed.*, p. 17.

3. See 'Martinus Scriblerus, of the Poem', *Twick. Ed.*, p. 50.

to Mr. *Savage* to desire him to give those verses another turn, to wit, "That *Pope* might now be the *first*, because *Moore* had left him unrival'd in turning his style to Comedy."[1]

By over-estimating their abilities the dunces are led to believe themselves good writers; convinced of this, they turn out writings which impose, Pope would have us believe, upon the 'honest and unpretending part of mankind', or conduce to the 'ruin or disturbance, of publick fame or private happiness'.[2] Pope apparently does not consider himself to be attacking sheer stupidity. As Cleland says, that amounts to a natural deformity over which a man has no control. The notes suggest increasingly that the satire is aimed at those who misuse whatever amount of sense they do possess (the dunces could not be improved simply by giving them *more* sense; they might still use it to wrong ends) and, by consequence, endanger the health of the culture in which they operate. Moreover, a dunce (as we shall more and more discover) is not to be defined as merely a poor writer or an unscrupulous publisher; wherever one finds presumption and the vain and unprincipled manipulation of even great capacities, there, too, Dulness will be Queen.

1. See note to II 46.
2. See *Twick. Ed.*, p. 17; see also note to II 149.

CHAPTER IV

A THEATRE FOR WORLDLINGS

I

IN 1742, thirteen years after the publication of the *Variorum*, Pope added a new book, the fourth,[1] to the *Dunciad*. Here the 'Removal' of the empire of duncery from the 'City' to the West End is seen as a *de facto* accomplishment, for the new book opens with a portrait of the Goddess Dulness as she ascends the throne in a court which appears to be a thinly-disguised imitation of St James's Palace:

> She mounts the Throne: her head a Cloud conceal'd,
> In broad Effulgence all below reveal'd,
> ('Tis thus aspiring Dulness ever shines)
> Soft on her lap her Laureat son reclines.
> Beneath her foot-stool, *Science* groans in Chains,
> And *Wit* dreads Exile, Penalties and Pains.
> There foam'd rebellious *Logic*, gagg'd and bound,
> There, stript, fair *Rhet'ric* languish'd on the ground . . .
>
> (IV 17–24)[2]

The occasion of the book is apparently that of a royal levee at which titles and degrees in duncery are awarded to all those who have helped, in whatever capacity, to make Dulness the highest power in the land. Before the new sovereign parade a highly diversified array of characters—fops, pedants, opera singers, virtuosi, deists, and coin collectors—to receive recognition for their part in the revolution which has exalted Dulness and placed the forces of order and right reason in bondage at her feet.

Book IV, like the *Variorum* notes, is not, finally, an addition

1. Called *The New Dunciad* and published separately. All four books were unified in 1743 and entitled *The Greater Dunciad*. Henceforth, because of the selectivity required in the discussion of certain matters, the line references in my text will be qualified by the letters 'A' or 'B', denoting the A (1729) or B (1743) texts of the Twickenham Edition of the *Dunciad*.
2. See the whole passage, *Twick. Ed.*, pp. 341–5.

thoroughly integrated with the original version of the poem. In some ways the additional book is superior in artistic achievement to the original poem, but it is questionable whether it is finally either a whole in itself or a fully integrated part. It is indeed sewn tightly and closely to the first three books, but the seaming still reveals itself. All four books deal with basically the same satiric subject matter, and in some ways Pope carries over into Book IV themes he had developed earlier (the scene in St James's is, for example, the climax of that movement from the City to the West End). But some evidence of the discontinuity between the books is seen in the fact that the parody of the 'action' of the *Aeneid* is not carried over, in any organic fashion, into Book IV. More important for our purposes is the change in artistic method one discovers in Book IV, and the change in tone which results from this different method. This change is seen, as I have already suggested, in the more dramatic presentation of the dunces' folly. The dunces reveal more in action and in speech their follies; Pope validates, in more immediate and dramatic fashion, his criticism of the dunces *in the poem*. Too often in the earlier books the poet presented the dunces merely as so many grotesque and dirty symbols, upon which he later had to elaborate in his notes. The satire of the Fourth Book is not less energetic than that of the first three, but the tone itself is far more healthy (certainly less personal and abusive) as a result of this change in technique.

Some of the more dramatic qualities of Book IV may derive from the source material used therein by Pope. Tracing the dramatic design of the Fourth Book, George Sherburn has suggested that Pope was indebted to several of Henry Fielding's farces for its structural plan. He points out that Fielding in 'two or three very popular farces had shown royal levees crammed with incongruous episodes that followed each other kaleidoscopically much as do the passages of Book IV', and that in both the *Dunciad* and Fielding's farces one finds a mock queen or goddess 'the focal point about which farcical episode may loosely revolve'.[1]

1. George Sherburn, 'The *Dunciad*, Book IV', *University of Texas Studies in English*, 24 (1944), pp. 180, 179.

The dramatic situation in Book IV seems indebted to other literary conventions too. One of these is that represented by the 'session' poem, a genre marked by assemblies of poets, musicians, critics, and the like, before the throne of Apollo. Such poems were also characterized, as is the *Dunciad*, by numerous speeches, comic or otherwise, on the part of these personages. In addition, awards were usually given by Apollo to his most favoured adherents on such occasions. Another convention stems from the seventeenth- and eighteenth-century imitations of an ancient ethical treatise called the 'Tablet of Cebes', a work in which appear various female personages of allegorical significance who are flanked in statuesque fashion by symbolic attendants. The 'Tablet', a thorough-going Socratic allegory, illustrates the follies and illusions which may beset the man who seeks a life of virtue. Pope mentions the 'Tablet' in a note to l. 153 of Book IV, and there appears to be a close resemblance between contemporary literary portraits modelled on the 'Tablet' and Pope's portrait of Dulness on her throne surrounded by her symbolic attendants.[1]

In any event, it is in Book IV that Pope most successfully creates a stage full of colourful personalities who have their dramatic entrances and exits, who hold the centre of the stage for a brief moment, and then are shoved aside by others. As William Ayre, a contemporary of Pope, remarked, in this book the 'Stage is full of the Goddess' Votaries'. And Ayre goes on to say that in this book too Pope has most effectively 'follow'd the dramatick Rule, of shewing the Humour of each Character the stronger, by shewing a contrast Character to it'.[2] Coming to the forefront, these characters are alternately tittering, surly, tearful in their declamations. And all the characters finally co-operate in the spectacle of a stage full of fools, more representative of human life than might at first appear.

As the richly clad and loquacious dunces parade to the fore and indulge in their manifold vanities the reader is given an in-

1. For a more extended discussion of the *Dunciad's* relationship to the 'sessions' poems and to the 'Tablet of Cebes', see my essay, 'Literary Backgrounds to Book Four of the *Dunciad*', *PMLA*, 68 (1953), pp. 806–13.
2. *Memoirs of the Life and Writings of Alexander Pope* (London, 1745), II 241, 243–4.

sight into their performance which is analogous to dramatic
irony. The insight is provided of course by the same uncritical
self-display we associated with Scriblerus and which Warton
found so disturbing in the dunces as a group. Unaware of the
vanity in which they are involved the actors are made to pro-
claim their own dulness. By this procedure the dunces appear
not so much damned by Pope as by themselves. In this fashion
there is revealed to us the arrogant pride of Bentley in his Di-
gamma, that of Montalto in his edition of Shakespeare; the pride
of the Governor in his pupil, 'A dauntless infant! never scared
with God', that of the antiquaries in their coins, of the virtuosi in
their flowers and butterflies, that of the 'gloomy Clerk' in—just
himself.

In only a few instances are real names used in Book IV, and a
positive identification of the pseudonyms—Annius, Silenus,
Paridel, and the like—with real persons is often impossible. The
sweep and diversity of the episodes, the anonymity of the actors
under their trappings of folly, the variety of emotions—anger
and sorrow, gaiety and gravity, the pageantry of the procession,
all suggest that the play of life in this book is an emblem of the
greater human spectacle, a 'dramatic' imitation thoroughly representative of the human situation. In this book we easily perceive the ordinary human weaknesses in which the dunces
share. We even perceive the underlying human tragedy in this
great scene, for it is a complex representation of man distracted
by vanities and urged into folly by the typical emotional and
intellectual compulsions of ordinary life. In this book a vision is
offered the reader of men still, as they are bound to be, by themselves abused, a vision of some of life's poor players, strutting and
fretting away their hours on stage.

II

The original three-book version of the *Dunciad*, though lacking in certain of the more 'dramatic' qualities which characterize
Book IV, is yet related, by Pope's use of metaphor, to the idea of
stage and theatre. In the first three books, for example, one is
reminded of the pantomimic activity which burdened the Lon-

don stages. We behold, with Theobald[1] in Book III, the 'scene she [Dulness] draws',[2] and witness a series of episodic situations which might have been taken from the very Smithfield farces the poem celebrates. There are young Theophilus Cibber

> who takes the foremost place,
> And thrusts his person full into your face;   (III 131–2 A)

the stage antics of Rich, who

> sits at ease
> Mid snows of paper, and fierce hail of pease;
> (III 257–8 A)

the lugubrious stage presence of 'two slip-shod Muses' who

> traipse along,
> In lofty madness, meditating song,
> With tresses staring from poetic dreams,
> And never wash'd, but in Castalia's streams.
> (III 141–4 A)

In Book II the dunces rush on stage like a troupe of buffoons:

> Now thousand tongues are heard in one loud din:
> The Monkey-mimicks rush discordant in.
> 'Twas chatt'ring, grinning, mouthing, jabb'ring all.
> (II 227–9 A)

In Book I there is the figurative choreography which Dulness 'Beholds thro' fogs that magnify the scene'[3]:

1. Theobald was replaced by Colley Cibber as King of Dunces in 1743. For convenience I use, for the greater part, the earlier monarch in this chapter.
2. Referring, as Sutherland notes (*Twick. Ed.*, p. 160, note to l. 119), to the scene disclosed when a stage curtain is drawn.
3. Cf. I 78 A. 'Scene' has its theatrical sense here. Such lines as these also extend the theatrical connotations:
> 'Tis yours [the dunces'] to shake the soul
> With thunder rumbling from the mustard-bowl,
> With horns and trumpets now to madness swell,
> Now sink in sorrows with a tolling Bell.
> Such happy arts attention can command,
> When fancy flags, and sense is at a stand.
> Improve we these. Three cat-calls be the bribe . . .

(II 217–23 A)
The thunder, 'tolling Bell', and cat-calls are all terms concerned with the stage, as is the passage at large. Cf. notes to the lines, *Twick. Ed.*, pp. 127–8.

> There motley Images her fancy strike,
> Figures ill-pair'd, and Similes unlike.
> She sees a Mob of Metaphors advance,
> Pleas'd with the Madness of the mazy dance.
>
> (I 63–6 A)

And in the following lines, which allude, Pope says, to 'the extravagancies of the Farces' written by Theobald,[1] we see

> Gods with Daemons in strange league ingage,
> And earth, and heav'n, and hell her [Dulness'] battles
> wage.   (I 107–8 A)

There are other elements which co-operate with the references to Smithfield farces and increase the poem's suggestions of the theatrical and spectacular. One of these is the mock-coronation of Theobald and the mock-royal procession which celebrates the new sovereign's accession to the throne[2]:

> Lift up your gates, ye Princes, see him come!
> Sound, sound ye Viols, be the Cat-call dumb!
> Bring, bring the madding Bay, the drunken Vine;
> The creeping, dirty, courtly Ivy join.
> And thou! his Aid de camp, lead on my sons,
> Light-arm'd with Points, Antitheses, and Puns.
> Let Bawdry, Billingsgate, my daughters dear,
> Support his front, and Oaths bring up the rear:
> And under his, and under Archer's[3] wing,
> Gaming and Grub-street skulk behind the King.
>
> (I 301–10 B)

The background provided by the Lord Mayor's Day celebration likewise contributes to an effect of rich pageantry in the poem:

> Pomps without guilt, of bloodless swords and maces,
> Glad chains, warm furs, broad banners, and broad faces.
>
> (I 85–6 A)

---

1. See *Twick. Ed.*, p. 76, note to l. 106. Theobald's *Rape of Proserpine* exemplifies this and other actions of the type Pope is here satirizing.

2. The mock-coronation elements recall Dryden's *Mac Flecknoe*.

3. Thomas Archer, Groom-Porter to Anne, George I, and George II. See *Twick. Ed.*, p. 292, note to ll. 309, 310.

> A motley mixture! in long wigs, in bags,
> In silks, in crapes, in garters, and in rags;
> From drawing rooms, from colleges, from garrets,
> On horse, on foot, in hacks, and gilded chariots.
>
> (II 17–20 A)

These suggestions of the 'theatrical', or of the spectacular, have two main functions in Pope's poem. On the one hand, they create a vivid scenario and convey what Lovejoy has called the Augustan delight in the world's 'infinite richness and diversity as a spectacle, the prodigious sweep of the complex and often tragic drama which it exhibits'.[1] On the other hand, they enable Pope to body forth again in striking and spectacular fashion the kind of intimate union between art and morality his age believed to exist. The 'artistic' activities of the 'monkey-mimicks' who grin, mouth, chatter, and jabber on the stage, or of the theatre-manager Rich, who on his Smithfield stage 'rides in the whirl-wind, and directs the storm', are used by Pope to suggest the kind of intellectual and moral confusion which duncery produces. The 'art' of the Smithfield theatre, the 'art' of the Lord Mayor's pageantry, the 'art' of the royal procession are made to image a kind of grotesque debasement of the human spirit.

The theatrical and spectacular elements pervade the whole of Pope's poem and finally exist in it in the form of a general atmospheric pressure. In one important place in the *Dunciad*, however, Pope uses a metaphor of the theatre in a particularly precise and crucial way. This shift in the poem from a general theatrical atmosphere to a charged theatrical metaphor occurs near the end of Book III when Theobald is given a vision of a 'new world' to be created in the future by the Goddess Dulness, a vision which is conveyed by a description of contemporary London stage practice and machinery. In other words, this vision is imaginatively presented through a skilful assemblage of concrete theatrical particulars—stage properties, stage personalities, farcical plots. Such materials are used by Pope as images to mirror a greater world, the 'real' world of human affairs. Since the pursuits of the duncies, by subverting existing standards and

1. A. O. Lovejoy, *The Great Chain of Being* (Cambridge, Mass., Harvard University Press, 1948), p. 189.

values, all tend toward the realization of some kind of 'new world', this vision of its 'creation' is crucial to the whole poem. It is exactly here, too, that we find the action of the poem most deeply involved in theatrics, that we see the stage as a metaphoric microcosm, and theatrical phenomena as symbolic of events in a moral and philosophic area.

At the heart of this metaphor of the theatre which Pope creates lies the ancient classical view that God, the stage manager, has assigned to men certain roles to play on the stage of the world—a 'calling' in the older sense of the word. Man's duty is to play his part well, to make the best of whatever lot he has, and not to rebel against the Author by desiring another, more exalted, role, or by refusing the station assigned. 'Providence', as Simplicius comments, 'hath appointed our Character, and we cannot change or decline it'.[1] Or as Epictetus puts it in the passage Simplicius glosses:

> Remember, that the World is a Theatre, and that your Part in this Play of Life is determined by the Poet. Upon him it must depend, whether you shall act a long or a short one: whether your Character shall be high or low: If therefore he assign you that of a Beggar, take care to humour it well; if a Cripple, or a Prince, or a private obscure Man, or whatever it be, make the best of it: For consider, that the playing of the Part assigned you commendably, depends upon yourself. This is your Business: but the giving out of the Parts, and chusing the Actors, is not Yours, but another Person's.[2]

The cause of an attempt to transcend one's status, to shed one role for another, is 'pride' or 'presumption', while the effect is to bring confusion into God's ordered plan, to spoil the play of life for the other actors. Here, of course, we should recall that it was the pretensions of the duncees to poetic status that provided Pope with the moral justification of his satire. By over-estimating their abilities, the duncees were led to believe themselves good writers and, as a result, produced an effect (their writings)

---

1. *Epictetus His Morals, With Simplicius His Comment,* trans. by George Stanhope, 5th edn (London, 1741), p. 123.
2. Ibid. Cf. *An Essay on Man,* IV 194: 'Act well your part: there all the honour lies'.

which imposed, as the Cleland letter says, upon the 'honest and unpretending part of mankind'. In Pope's view the dunces should have been content with roles for which they were better fitted. Theobald, presumably, should have remained an attorney, Ned Ward a bar-tender, Blackmore a physician.

The connection of Theobald's vision with the tradition of viewing the stage as emblematic of the greater world can be introduced best, perhaps, by a humorous passage from one of the *Spectator* papers which may have served as source for this part of Pope's poem:

> I look upon the play-house as a world within itself. They have lately furnished the middle region of it with a new set of meteors, in order to give the sublime to many modern tragedies. I was there last winter at the first rehearsal of the new thunder, which is much more deep and sonorous that any hitherto made use of. They have a Salmoneus behind the scenes, who plays it off with great success. Their lightnings are made to flash more briskly than heretofore; their clouds are also better furbelowed, and more voluminous; not to mention a violent storm locked up in a great chest that is designed for the Tempest. They are also provided with above a dozen showers of snow, which, as I am informed, are the plays of many unsuccessful poets artificially cut and shredded for that use.[1]

In the following lines from the *Dunciad* we see John Rich, the theatre manager, as he manipulates his stage machinery for the creation of a proper stage scene, or theatrical 'world', of a farce. Here he is, like the Salmoneus[2] in the *Spectator* passage, at his playhouse task, giving his audience at Lincoln's Inn Fields (and ultimately the reader of the *Dunciad*) the illusion of events in a greater order:

> In yonder cloud, behold!
> Whose sarcenet skirts are edg'd with flamy gold,
> A matchless Youth: His nod these worlds controuls,

1. No. 592 (Friday, 10 September).
2. Pope gives this note to his lines: 'Like *Salmoneus* in *Æn*. 6 [586, 590–1].
   Dum flammas Jovis, & sonitus imitatur Olympi.
   —Nimbos, & non imitabile fulmen,
   Ære & cornipedum cursu simularat aequorum.'

> Wings the red lightning, and the thunder rolls.
> Angel of Dulness, sent to scatter round
> Her magic charms o'er all unclassic ground:
> Yon stars, yon suns, he rears at pleasure higher,
> Illumes their light, and sets their flames on fire.
> Immortal Rich! how calm he sits at ease
> Mid snows of paper, and fierce hail of pease;
> And proud his mistress' orders to perform,
> Rides in the whirlwind, and directs the storm.
>
> (III 249–60 A)

Though on one level the lines serve mainly to remind us of the type of 'show' current in the London theatres, on another they contain more sinister implications. The tinselled stars and gilded suns of the backdrop, the artificial thunder and lightning, the playhouse itself, all begin to appear as phenomena in a 'real' universe. The local (the London theatres), the literary (the shredded poetic snows), the temporary (farcical pantomime), fuse into an image of what will happen when the forces of Dulness finally triumph and her 'angels' re-create the 'world' in her image. Here we see how the stage has actually evolved into a chaotic 'new world' of Dulness:

> He look'd, and saw a sable Sorc'rer rise,
> Swift to whose hand a winged volume flies:
> All sudden, Gorgons hiss, and Dragons glare,
> And ten-horn'd fiends and Giants rush to war,
> Hell rises, Heav'n descends, and dance on Earth,
> Gods, imps, and monsters, music, rage, and mirth,
> A fire, a jig, a battle, and a ball,
> Till one wide Conflagration swallows all.
>   Thence a new world, to Nature's laws unknown,
> Breaks out refulgent, with a heav'n its own:
> Another Cynthia her new journey runs,
> And other planets circle other suns:
> The forests dance, the rivers upward rise,
> Whales sport in woods, and dolphins in the skies,
> And last, to give the whole creation grace,
> Lo! one vast Egg produces human race. (III 229–44 A)

In his notes Pope explains that the lines reflect the stage extravagancies of his day. The 'one wide conflagration' which swallows all is a humorous allusion, probably, to the occasions when, as in the performance of Theobald's *Rape of Proserpine*, 'a Cornfield was set on fire', or when a barn was burnt on stage (to rival Theobald's blaze).[1] But the passage also images, in mock-apocalyptic fashion, the final destruction of the real world: stage anarchy is made to carry a vision of chaos in the natural order. For in the mirror that a shapeless and lawless art holds up to nature, nature is bound to appear shapeless and lawless too.

The point of real importance then is the fact that in these stage scenes, however trivial their particulars, Pope conveys to the reader the fancy that Dulness and her agents are dedicated to the destruction of one order and to the miscreation of a new. Other implications of the profanation wrought by Dulness also filter through when we note the theological resonances, many of them deriving from Revelation: the 'ten-horn'd fiends', the 'Dragon', the final 'Conflagration'. These recall the earthly ruin brought about by Satan, while the 'new world . . . with a heav'n its own' suggests, in a manner that attaches still further impiety to the acts of Dulness, the 'new heaven and new earth' which Christ will cause to spring from the ruined world.[2] In the same way, Rich's act of hanging the stars and suns in his theatrical firmament is made to parody the original creation of the heavenly lights. About the whole scene clings an aura of disorder and impiety. The cluttered huddle of the verse in such lines as 'Gods, imps, and monsters, music, rage, and mirth, / A fire, a jig, a battle, and a ball' suggests a totally disordered universe, while Rich, as the Angel of Dulness, recalls that 'Angel of Light' into which Lucifer converted himself. Similarly, the parody of Virgil's Salmoneus, a rebel against Jove who sought to take the divine powers into his own hands, deepens the context of profanation, as do the parodies of *Paradise Lost*, reminding us of the heavenly war between the good and bad angels:

> But lo! to dark encounter in mid air[3]
> New wizards rise: here Booth, and Cibber there:

1. See *Twick. Ed.*, p. 185, note to l. 310.   2. See Revelation, xxi 1.
3. Cf. *P.L.*, II 718, where Satan and Death prepare 'To joyn thir dark Encounter in mid air'.

> Booth in his cloudy tabernacle shrin'd,[1]
> On grinning dragons Cibber mounts the wind:
> Dire is the conflict, dismal is the din,[2]
> Here shouts all Drury, there all Lincoln's-Inn;
> Contending Theatres our empire raise . . .
>
> (III 261–7 A)

At points like these, the *Dunciad* rises to another level of meaning. Simultaneous with the removal of the empire of Dulness from the City to the Court there occurs a sublimer metaphoric 'action': the transformation of Dulness into a preternatural concentrate of mortal duncery who, operating through her instruments, the dunces,[3] deranges order in literature, in society, and finally in the whole world. Pope conveys this conception by having us view the stage as a 'world within itself', as Addison said, a universe in microcosm, and by using Smithfield theatrics—farcical stage antics, the plays of the dunces— to represent the kind of anarchic dominion a reign of Dulness would entail.

Pope's theatrical representation of a world of Dulness thus exists primarily to mirror and measure the broad moral and cultural upheaval of his own time.[4] The chaotic 'nature' of Dulness, where 'Whales sport in woods' and the 'rivers upward rise', is the physical image of a world where 'Eusden wears the bays', Ambrose Philips is 'prefer'd for Wit', and 'Gay dies unpension'd with a hundred Friends'. The single vision (of uncreation and creation) is an imaginative device whose function is to 'con-

1. An inversion of *P.L.*, VII 248.
2. Cf. *P.L.*, VI 211–13:   . . . dire was the noise
                     Of conflict; over head the dismal hiss
                     Of fiery Darts . . .

3. Cf. the last line of the preceding quotation:
                     Contending Theatres our empire raise.

4. Consider Pope's comment on these lines:
                     Then rose the Seed of Chaos, and of Night,
                     To blot out Order, and extinguish Light,
                     Of dull and venal a new World to mold,
                     And bring Saturnian days of Lead and Gold.   (IV 13–16)
". . . *a new World*] In allusion to the Epicurean opinion, That from the Dissolution of the natural World into Night and Chaos, a new one should arise; this the Poet alluding to, in the Production of a new moral World, makes it partake of its original Principles."

cretize' sweeping alterations[1] in the more intangible world of values.

Throughout the *Dunciad* Pope increases the freight his metaphors of art and theatre can carry by endowing the inanimate, the local, the literary, with a new quality of being. He 'humanizes' journals, odes, pamphlets, and transforms (as we have seen) stage machinery into the 'nature' of a created universe. This process deepens and enriches his whole conception of a new 'world' of Dulness; mere 'things' become, like the dunces, moral agents: odes that dance, plays that copulate, stage dragons that seem 'alive'. The general animation tends to make this world of bad art vividly applicable to the world of human values.

Walter Harte seems to have understood this procedure of endowing the inanimate with animate, organic 'being'. Speaking of the *Dunciad*, he noted

> It gives not *Things*, but *Beings* to our eyes,
> *Life*, *Substance*, *Spirit*, animate the whole;
> *Fiction* and *Fable* are the Sense and Soul.
> The *common Dulness* of mankind, array'd
> In pomp, here lives and breathes, a *wond'rous Maid*.[2]

Nor need we take 'being' in this passage as entirely excluding that sense so congenial in the eighteenth century and earlier, the ontological sense in which God is pure 'Being', and His Creation a graduated scale of communicated 'being'. At any rate, there is more than one hint in Pope's poem that as God is immanent in His creation, Dulness is immanent in hers, down to the last birthday ode. Thus in Book I Dulness 'her wild creation views', beholds a 'scene' of 'Maggots half-form'd' that 'learn to crawl upon poetic feet', sees a 'Mob of Metaphors advance, Pleas'd

1. Just how sweeping are the alterations Pope supposes is indicated by the extended note to ll. 76–101 of Book IV. There the view of the changes becomes 'cosmological', and the poet draws an explicit parallel between his metaphor of creation and events in what he again calls 'the moral world'. Such analogies between the moral and physical orders were not unusual in the age. Cf. *The Works of the Late Right Honourable Henry St. John, Lord Viscount Bolingbroke* (London, 1809), VIII, p. 232.

2. P. 6 of *An Essay on Satire*, in Richard Savage's *A Collection of Pieces in Verse and Prose, Which have been publish'd on Occasion of the DUNCIAD*.

with the madness of the mazy dance', watches while 'Tragedy and Comedy embrace', while 'Farce and Epic get a jumbled race', and founds her seat of empire amid 'Journals, Medleys, Merc'ries, Magazines', 'New-year Odes'—all the 'Grub-street race'.[1] To the same end, Cibber addresses the works he is about to sacrifice as 'real' offspring: 'O born in sin, and forth in folly brought!'[2] The daily papers are represented as 'a feeble, but a desp'rate pack, / With each a sickly brother at his back',[3] while the souls of unborn dunces

> Demand new bodies, and in Calf's array,[4]
> Rush to the world, impatient for the day.
>
> (III 29–30 B)

Pope's endowment of his playhouse 'world' with animate 'being' is singularly in keeping with the tradition of viewing the world as a stage. This tradition, as we have seen, placed great emphasis on man's keeping to the role assigned to him by God, the divine stage manager. It asserted, moreover, that any attempt to transcend one's given role was an act of pride. This traditional perspective on man has its counterpart in an ethics derived from contemporary reflection on the chain of being. Lovejoy states the ethical implications this way: 'Since every place in the scale [of being] must be filled, and since each is what it is by virtue of the special limitations which differentiate it from any other, man's duty was to keep *his* place, and not to seek to transcend it—which, nevertheless, he was characteristically prone to do'.[5] It is scarcely by chance that Bolingbroke, in a brief passage which appears almost like an exposition of Pope's 'world', should bring together in synthesis the two elements of 'stage metaphor' and 'scale of being'. Bolingbroke shows how each perspective strengthened and collaborated with the other,

---

1. See I 82 B, I 61–2 B, I 67–70 B, I 42, 44 B.   2. I 225 B.
3. II 305–6 B.
4. Pope says (*Twick. Ed.*, p. 152, note to l. 20), 'The Allegory of the souls of the Dull coming forth in the form of Books drest in calve's leather, and being let abroad in vast numbers by Booksellers, is sufficiently intelligible.' In his animation of books, Pope had the precedent of Swift in the *Battle of the Books* as well as of a number of other works.
5. *The Great Chain of Being*, p. 200.

and places, moreover, his finger on the disorder introduced, into both contexts, by presumption:

> The whole world, nay the whole universe *is filled with beings*, which are all connected in one immense design. The sensitive inhabitants of our globe, *like the dramatis personae*, have different characters, and are applied to different purposes of *action in every scene*. The several parts of the material world, *like the machines of a theatre*, were contrived *not for the actors*, but for the action: and the *whole order and system of the drama would be disordered and spoiled*, if any alteration was made in either. The nature of every creature, *his manner of being*, is adapted to his stage here, to the place he is to inhabit, and, as we may say, *to the part he is to play*.[1]

One could hardly ask for a better gloss to Pope's theatrical world of 'being'. Even the 'machines of a theatre' are employed in precisely the metaphoric manner in which Pope deals with the stage paraphernalia of Rich. And the passage makes clear the net of moral and philosophical assumptions in which the poet has caught the dunces' efforts to mar a sacrosanct polity in art and society.

Reflection on the scale of being led Pope and his contemporaries to regard Pride as the 'sin "against the laws of order"', i.e., of gradation [of being]'. Pride represented 'an attempt "to counterwork the Eternal Cause", to disturb the very system of the universe'.[2] In other poems, too, Pope concerned himself with the effect of pride on the hierarchy of beings:

> In pride, in reas'ning pride, our error lies;
> All quit their sphere, and rush into the skies!
> Pride still is aiming at the bless'd abodes,
> Men would be Angels, Angels would be Gods.
> <div align="right">(<i>An Essay on Man</i>, 1 123–6)</div>

1. *Works* (London, 1809), VIII, p. 232, italics mine. This passage is from *Fragments or Minutes of Essays*, which Bolingbroke could not have written before 1731 (see Maynard Mack's introduction to *An Essay on Man*, Twickenham Edition, London, Methuen & Co., 1950; New Haven, Yale University Press, 1951, pp. xxix ff.). Since *An Essay on Man* probably influenced the phrasing of the *Fragments*, it may be that this portion of the *Dunciad* (which Bolingbroke would almost surely have interpreted much as I am trying to do) did also.   2. Lovejoy, *The Great Chain of Being*, p. 201.

And the poet expounds the same text in the *Dunciad*: the actions of Rich, that agent of folly who has rushed into the skies to become the

> Angel of Dulness, sent to scatter round
> Her magic charms o'er all unclassic ground,

are a dramatic anticipation of the passage in *An Essay on Man*, while the satanic complex in which Rich is environed ultimately suggests that his activity on behalf of Dulness *is* an attempt to 'counterwork the Eternal Cause'.

Theobald's vision of the future world of Dulness flows almost immediately (in the earlier, three-book, versions of the poem) into an even grander imaginative event; what was only prophesied to the King of Dunces starts to become, at the close of the poem, a 'reality'. Here Pope's use of artistic deterioration as suggestive of moral and spiritual deterioration reaches a climax. In the conclusion of the 1728 version the meaning gradually expands from the local and aesthetic (laureates, architecture, duncical wit, the trials of Gay and Swift) to the consummate inversion of creation expressed in

> Let there be darkness! (the dread pow'r shall say)
> All shall be darkness, as it ne'er were Day.[1]

In the 1729 version of the poem, new and more important realms of value wither before the advance of the Goddess Dulness to a kind of cosmic dominion:

> She comes! the Cloud-compelling Pow'r, behold!
> With Night Primaeval, and with Chaos old.
> Lo! the great Anarch's ancient reign restor'd,
> Light dies before her uncreating word:
> As one by one, at dread Medaea's strain,
> The sick'ning Stars fade off th' aethereal plain;
> As Argus' eyes, by Hermes' wand opprest,
> Clos'd one by one to everlasting rest;
> Thus at her felt approach, and secret might,
> Art after Art goes out, and all is Night.
> See sculking Truth in her old cavern lye,

1. See variant reading, *Twick. Ed.*, p. 192.

> Secur'd by mountains of heap'd casuistry:
> Philosophy, that touch'd the Heavens before,
> Shrinks to her hidden cause, and is no more:
> See Physic beg the Stagyrite's defence!
> See Metaphysic call for aid on Sence!
> See Mystery to Mathematicks fly!
> In vain! they gaze, turn giddy, rave, and die.
>
> (III 337–54 A)

And with a final reminder of the theatrical nature of the scenes we have been witnessing, both early versions of the poem conclude:

> Thy hand great Dulness! lets the curtain fall,
> And universal Darkness covers all.

From the apparently insignificant sufferings of a Gay or Swift amidst the local dulness of contemporary officialdom, the conclusion progrésses line by line in an ever-growing revelation of the ultimate consequences for truth, morality, philosophy, and religion, in a world conquered by Dulness's prevenient grace.

H

CHAPTER V

OF WISDOM—AND DULNESS

INTO the fourth book of the *Dunciad* that was 'found' and first published in 1742 Pope packed a whole world of traditional ethical and philosophical ideas and attitudes. Often there is distilled into a couplet the essence of an idea that had ramified for generations in the history of moral philosophy. This procedure, which introduces into the poem backgrounds quite distinct from any we have hitherto discussed, gives Book IV great richness of meaning at the same time that it creates a practically endless exegetical task. Such condensation is bound to occur, of course, in a good satirical poem: the satirist's province is not philosophic elaboration, but the branding of deviations from various norms. A phrase or couplet may be enough to invoke a conception of the norm violated, the philosophic or religious background against which a type of folly is to be viewed. It is the aim of this chapter to re-create, in some degree, this 'world' of tradition so powerfully condensed in Book IV.

I

For a proper perspective on the *Dunciad*'s position in literary history it should be understood first of all that the Battle between Ancients and Moderns is perennial—and that Pope's war against duncery is but one campaign in that enduring struggle. To use the words 'ancient' and 'modern' is, in fact, to risk a blurring of the issues, for the terms too often appear to restrict the strife to a certain period of time—the seventeenth and eighteenth centuries. The War of the Dunces (and that of the Ancients and Moderns) is best described, perhaps, as one waged between eighteenth-century versions of humanist and schoolman. To describe the fray in these terms is to see the parties involved as standing on either side of a cleavage in thought and attitude which extends through the whole of Western civilization: the labels applied to the opposing parties change, but the parties contend about the same issues.

At the heart of the struggle is the concern with the means, use, ends, limits of human knowledge, and the most helpful approach to this problem, in the light of both the contemporary educational situation and the poem itself, may be made, perhaps, through the medium of two parts of the *trivium*—rhetoric and dialectic. Set in the light of these disciplines, the controversy between the Ancients and Moderns, between Pope and Swift and the dunces, will begin to appear, in some respects, as a resumption, or continuation, of the controversies between the Sophists and Plato, between Cicero and the philosophers, between the humanists and the schoolmen, between the poets and the virtuosi of the seventeenth century.[1]

The issues of the struggle are raised best by viewing each of the contending parties through the eyes of its opponent. To the dialectician, the logician, the scientist and virtuoso, the 'art' of rhetoric quite often, in Plato's terms, becomes little more than an art of cookery, serving up seasonable sauces to titillate the appetites of an audience,[2] not so much concerned with delivering the naked truth as with clouding the issues or functioning for self-display.[3] The boast of the Sophists, that wisdom could be taught by words, met stubborn denunciation from Plato and Aristotle. And there is, of course, always the danger in any rhetoric of a degeneration into mere words, empty and meaningless verbalism. To the scientist and the logician, who are more interested in things, in the matter, than in words, and who wish to express 'So many things, almost in an equal number of words'

1. I am indebted to the unpublished doctoral dissertation of Mr Marshall McLuhan, 'The Place of Thomas Nashe in the Learning of His Time' (submitted in 1943 to Cambridge University), for much of my knowledge of the background of this section. The third part of the *trivium*, grammar, though it had a great role in earlier controversies, is, for various reasons, not so important by the time of Pope. See below, however, p. 119–21, for some discussion of its relation to Pope's campaign against the dunces.

2. Bacon remarks on the analogy: 'And therefore it was great injustice in Plato, though springing out of a just hatred to the rhetoricians of his time, to esteem of rhetoric but as a voluptuary art, resembling it to cookery, that did mar wholesome meats, and help unwholesome by variety of sauces to the pleasure of the taste'. *The Advancement of Learning*, ed. W. A. Wright (Oxford, 1869), p. 178.

3. Cf. C. S. Baldwin, *Medieval Rhetoric and Poetic* (New York, The Macmillan Company, 1928), pp. 2–5.

(as the members of the Royal Society desired to do), the function of rhetoric may appear slight indeed.

Doubtless many modern readers—detached from the rhetorical tradition almost entirely—would accept readily the attitude of the rational inquirer. But if such a reader properly understands the concept of verbal wisdom as preached by Cicero and inherited by the Renaissance, he may soon find himself beset with misgivings. 'The training of the public speaker, this tradition consistently repeats, must focus the whole training of the man'.[1] In the hands of a Cicero,[2] a St Augustine,[3] an Ascham, the *doctus orator* becomes the perfect expression of a Roman and Renaissance ideal: the well-rounded man who can put his knowledge to use on behalf of the commonweal. The ideal man of the Renaissance and of Augustan England (this is implicit in the analogies constantly drawn by the Augustans between themselves and the men of ancient Rome) was a man of learning and of moral and civil perspicacity who, above all else, found the outlet for his capacities in the realm of civil prudence. To the formation of such a man the rhetorical discipline was dedicated. Eloquence, as the age regarded it, was the art by which knowledge of matters both spiritual and temporal was oriented toward the betterment of society, by which men were trained to be useful and moral citizens. Eloquence was in fact to be looked upon 'as a *political accomplishment*'.[4] To the humanist, the 'ancient' of the seventeenth and the poet of the eighteenth centuries (to all those whose wisdom had not been lost in know-

1. C. S. Baldwin, *Ancient Rhetoric and Poetic* (New York, The Macmillan Company, 1924), p. 40.
2. 'For after all the foundation of eloquence, as of everything else, is wisdom'. *Orator*, trans. by H. M. Hubbell, The Loeb Classical Library (Cambridge, Mass., Harvard University Press; London, William Heinemann Ltd, 1939), p. 357 (xx 70). In *de Oratore* (The Loeb Classical Library edition, trans. by E. W. Sutton and H. Rackham, Cambridge, Mass., Harvard University Press; London, William Heinemann Ltd, 1948), Book III xx, Cicero says oratory embraces 'all the virtues and duties, all the natural principles governing the morals and minds and life of mankind'.
3. Cf. *On Christian Doctrine*, well enough known in eighteenth-century England. See also Thomas Sheridan's *British Education, Or the Sources of the Disorders of Great Britain* (London, 1769), pp. 148–9.
4. Cf. William Guthrie's preface to his translation of *de Oratore* (London, 1755), p. x.

ledge, nor their knowledge in information), the schoolmen and the virtuosi were bound to appear mere rationalists or curious seekers after facts irrelevant to the true good of man and of society.[1] By the humanist the dialectician is likely to be described as the spider that spins forth 'cobwebs of learning, admirable for the fineness of thread and work, but of no substance or profit',[2] or as the silkworm that 'labours till it cloud itself all o'er' (*Dunciad*, IV 254).

From the time of Cicero, eloquence and wisdom had been considered by many as practically synonymous. The Augustan concept of 'wisdom' (a term which had, for the age, a quite specific content) is implicit in much of what has been said, but it may be well to state more precisely some of its implications.[3] Wisdom suggested, first of all, a life of active virtue;[4] it involved practice[5] rather more than theory—and not compartmentalized practice, but activity that included the whole man as a single moral, religious, and sentient being. Finally, 'wisdom' involved the *use* of learning for the benefit of others. The emphasis is on useful knowledge, but not 'useful' in the sense to which the virtuosi of the seventeenth century had attempted to narrow the term.[6] Utilitarian wisdom—which ministered to the needs and lusts of the body alone—was known as 'worldly wisdom' (i.e.,

1. For the most complete statement of the Augustan ideals in this respect, and one which states explicitly their relation to the art of oratory, see Sheridan, *British Education, passim*.

2. Bacon (*The Advancement of Learning*, p. 32) thus describes the schoolmen. The image is one of the most pervasive in the Renaissance period. Cf. Swift's spider in the *Battle of the Books*; also Pope's image in the *Essay on Criticism*:

> Scotists and Thomists now in peace remain
> Amidst their kindred cobwebs in Duck-lane.   (II 244–5)

3. Pierre Charron's three-volume work, *Of Wisdom*, represented for the age perhaps the most complete analysis of the meaning of 'wisdom'.

4. Cf. Quintilian's insistence that the orator be a 'good man'. *Institutio Oratoria*, III vii 25.

5. Cf. the view of Vives that the art of rhetoric 'arises out of practical wisdom'. Juan Luis Vives, *On Education*, a translation of *De Tradendis Disciplinis* by Foster Watson (Cambridge, Cambridge University Press, 1913), p. 39.

6. Cf. the protests made against the scientific appropriation of the term 'useful' by Meric Casaubon in *A Letter . . . to Peter du Moulin* (Cambridge, 1669), pp. 2, 4–7, 15, 31.

folly),[1] and was kept distinct from 'humane wisdom'—that wisdom which ministered to the needs of the whole man, his political, social, moral, and religious, as well as economic requirements.

With all these implications of 'wisdom' the rhetorical ideal harmonized perfectly. What distinguished the orator from the metaphysician and scientist was his ability to put his knowledge to use—the orator could communicate his wisdom, whereas the others were regarded by many in the age as full of reasoning and odd facts which they were unable, because of their 'crabbed' dialectic or scientific 'taciturnity' (Pope calls the virtuosi the 'silent Race'[2]), to put to use in the realm of civil affairs or for the advancement of real virtue. As John Brown declared, 'if we regard what is of more Importance to Man, than mere speculative Truth, I mean the *practical Ends* of human Life and moral Action; then Eloquence assumes a higher Nature . . .'[3]

To pin the label of '*rhetor*' on Pope would be of course a vast over-simplification of the actual facts, but what we can do to advantage is to regard him as a writer living within the humanist milieu of attitudes, a milieu which received its clearest expression in the Ciceronian ideal of the Renaissance, and which even in his own time was kept fresh by a constant influx from the same traditional well-spring. It was only natural that the supreme philosophy for Pope, as for his predecessors, should be moral philosophy, that he, like them, should favour 'humane wisdom' in opposition to what appeared to many as a proud scientism'.[4]

The very title of Pope's poem should have effected, long be-

1. Cf. Pierre Charron, *Of Wisdom*, trans. by George Stanhope, 3rd edn (London, 1729), I b2ᵛ.

2. IV 571, and note.

3. *Essays on the Characteristics*, 4th edn (London, 1755), pp. 30–1.

4. It is well to keep in mind that the first divorce of wisdom and knowledge, of knowledge and practice, was considered to be Satan's work: 'I cannot but bewaile . . . those two sad Divorces, that excellent French man, *Charron de la sagesse*, hath bewailed before mee: *viz.* Of Probity and Piety, coming from that first divorce of Knowledge and Practice, or (as he termeth them) *Science & Sagesse*, that is, Knowledge, and Wisdom.' '. . . since he [Satan] first divorced *knowledge* and *practice* in our first Parents, he is loath they should ever *marry* again.' See Richard Whitlock, *ZΩOTOMIA, or, Observations on the Present Manners of the English* (London, 1654), pp. 192–3, 138.

fore now, a recognition of the terms in which (on one of its levels at least) the battle is fought. Only R. K. Root and Émile Montégut have even considered the ancestry of the term 'dunce', and no one has seriously applied the term's suggestions to an interpretation of the poem. The word, as Root notes, is derived from the great schoolman, Duns Scotus, and was regularly applied by humanists to exponents of the scholastic philosophy. With the 'humanists of the sixteenth century it had taken on the sense of "cavilling sophist", "hair-splitting pedant". . . . As Pope uses the word, it suggests not stupidity or ignorance, but a perverse misapplication of intelligence, learning without wisdom, the precise opposite of all that is implied by the term "humanist"'.[1] For many of the newly literate of Pope's day, no doubt, the derivation of the word had little significance—just as, since Pope's time, the word seems to remind most readers mainly of a schoolboy in a pointed cap. But the writings of the seventeenth and eighteenth centuries give the term a specific sense, one designed to recall precisely those qualities that earlier humanists had found abhorrent. And along with 'dunce' there were a number of other epithets which set off those whom the age regarded as latter-day 'schoolmen', *viz.*, all those who misused their rational faculties, whether as virtuosi, grammarians, logicians, philosophers, or theologians. Thus Descartes is a 'modern schoolman'; the pedants and such logical grammarians as Bentley are 'speculative reasoners'; what is to be feared is 'northern barbarism', a second 'Gothic invasion' of learning. It is almost amusing, amidst all this, to observe William Wotton, a strident 'modern' and champion of 'neo-scholasticism', incautious, or

1. *The Dunciad Variorum* (Princeton, Princeton University Press, 1929), p. 15. See also Émile Montégut, 'Heures de Lecture d'un Critique—Pope', *Revue des Deux Mondes*, 86 (1888), p. 311 n. Here are three examples of a usage of the word 'dunce' spanning one hundred and fifty years. 'Heads were cast together, and Counsel devised, that *Duns*, with all the Rabble of barbarous Questionists, should have dispossessed of their Place and Room *Aristotle, Plato, Tully,* and *Demosthenes.*'—Ascham, *The Schoolmaster* (London, 1711), pp. 169–70. '. . . he came to *Doctor . . . per saltum,* or say some years of Duncery spent in a Gown, never had any thing in him *Magister Artium,* but his belly.'—Richard Whitlock, *ZΩOTOMIA* (London, 1654), p. 101. 'But Aristotle was out of all patience with the account I gave him of Scotus and Ramus . . . and he asked them whether the rest of the tribe were as great dunces as themselves'.—Swift, *Gulliver's Travels,* Chap. viii, Part iii.

bold enough, to claim the medieval schoolmen as members of the modern party.[1]

The foundation of wisdom was considered to be self-know-ledge,[2] a type of knowledge Pope indicates, throughout his poem, the dunces do not possess. The poet would have agreed with Shaftesbury that the 'super-speculative Philosophy' of the modern 'schoolmen' should be confronted 'with a more prac-tical sort, which relates chiefly to our Acquaintance, Friendship, and good Correspondence with *our-selves*'.[3] He would also have agreed with Shaftesbury that the knowledge of human nature and of one's self is the '*Philosophy*, which, by Nature, has the Pre-eminence above all other Science, or Knowledge':

> It has not its Name, as other Philosophys, from the mere Subtlety and Nicety of the Speculation; but, by way of Excel-lence, from its being superior to all other Speculations . . . She gives to every inferiour Science its just rank; leaves some to measure *Sounds*; others to scan *Syllables*; others to weigh *Vacuums*, and define *Spaces*, and *Extensions* . . .[4]

Instead of learning to know themselves, the dunces are shown in Book IV as running into one of two extremes: they fasten on external factual knowledge—the weeds and shells of the vir-tuosi; or they seek knowledge Pope regards as beyond man's capabilities—they rush into the skies to measure and define the Supreme Being. In either case they never learn the humility that comes through self-knowledge: they become, on the con-trary, knowledge-proud.

Pope did not appreciate sufficiently, one must admit, the very real values of experimental methods and of speculative reason-ing. At the same time it is possible to see that the poet was quite properly concerned (as subsequent events have shown) to pro-tect certain other areas of value from a threat created by ex-cesses in the use of such procedures. The whole problem is some-

1. 'It cannot be denied, but a good deal of this Methodical Exactness was at first owing to the School-men; but they are Moderns here . . .' See *Reflec-tions Upon Ancient and Modern Learning*, 3rd edn (London, 1705), p. 376.
2. Cf. the opening sentences of Charron's *Of Wisdom*.
3. *Characteristicks of Men, Manners, Opinions, Times*, 2nd edn, I, p. 292.
4. Ibid., pp. 297–8.

times dismissed by saying, with reference to Pope's satire on the virtuosi, that 'Gibes at the Royal Society were frequent among the wits'; or with reference to his criticism of speculation un-limited, that this illustrates the fashion of 'ridiculing Mathe-matics and mathematicians'.[1] But to do this is to fail to see what lies behind the fashion (if it was one), to ignore in men like Swift and Pope the keen awareness of their own intellectual position in the bitterly-contested struggle about the ends, use, and limits of human knowledge. It was certainly with the design of setting forth clearly his own position that Pope, in a letter to Swift,[2] proposed four Epistles

> which naturally follow the Essay on Man, *viz.* 1. Of the Extent and limits of Human Reason and Science. 2. A View of the useful and therefore attainable, and of the un-useful and therefore un-attainable, Arts. 3. Of the Nature, Ends, Applications, and Use of different Capacities. 4. Of the Use of *Learning*, of the *Science* of the *World*, and of *Wit*.

The epistles 'will conclude', the poet goes on to say, 'with a Satire against the mis-application of all these [human capaci-ties], exemplify'd by pictures, characters, and examples'. Frag-ments of these proposed epistles, it is generally agreed, found their way into Book IV of the *Dunciad*. Pope himself told Spence that 'What was first designed for an Epistle on Education, as part of my Essay-scheme, is now inserted in my Fourth Dun-ciad'.[3] For practical purposes, in fact, we may perhaps view Book IV as having accomplished, in however altered a form, most of Pope's plan. It *is* a satire against the 'mis-application of' human capacities, 'exemplify'd by pictures, characters, and examples'.

II

A concern for the rhetorical tradition which both sustained and, to a certain extent, defined Augustan humanism,[4] inevit-

1. *Twick. Ed.*, notes to IV 570, IV 31.   2. 25 March 1736.
3. Joseph Spence, *Observations, Anecdotes, and Characters, of Books and Men* (London, 1820), pp. 56–7.
4. Soon after Pope's death, Thomas Sheridan (1719–88) devoted an entire book (*British Education*, London, 1769) to the idea that the only hope for England was firm adherence to the study of oratory in English schools.

ably led Pope and others to a concern for the dignity and integrity of the 'word' itself. Because the humanist regarded the 'word' as 'wisdom' expressed, it was most important that he prevent a decline of rhetoric into mere verbalism. Corruption of this sort had for him consequences injurious to a whole body of related values, to society itself. And while Pope's antipathy to corrupters of the word is evident throughout the *Dunciad*, it is in Book IV that he most consistently contrasts (by the use of allusions which call to mind concepts and attitudes long ingrained in the rhetorical tradition) the Ciceronian ideal and the word-mongering of the dunces. Few instances of this opposition are more crucial than that revealed in the words of the 'master of public schools':

> Since Man from beast by Words is known,
> Words are Man's province, Words we teach alone.[1]
>
> (IV 149–50)

Here of course is a phrase of profoundest meaning for a humanist. The distinction between man and beast was presumed traditionally to reside in the faculty of speech,[2] though of course it was always understood that by 'speech' was implied 'reason'. Speech reproduced thought in words; words were the means by which truth and reason were communicated and by which men were bound together in society. But what the speaker here does is to ignore the content the humanists gave to the term 'words'; he would empty eloquence of its wisdom, squeeze out of the word the thought it was believed to embody:

> [We] confine the thought, to exercise the breath;
> And keep them in the pale of Words till death.

Although apparently aiming at education in style alone, the humanists, as S. S. Laurie says, really considered themselves to be giving education in the 'substance, as well as artistic form, of Literature'. Rhetorical discipline meant not '*merely* style or rhe-

---

1. 'I shall need no Allowance, I think, for saying that Boys learn nothing but Words, in the useful [*sic*, usual?] Method of the Schools . . .'—John Clarke, *An Essay Upon the Education of Youth in Grammar-Schools*, 2nd edn (London, 1730), p. 8.
2. Cf. Cicero, *de Oratore*, I viii.

toric, but the free unencumbered thought of reason on nature
and man'.[1] In the rhetorical discipline of the dull such 'unencumbered thought' is made impossible to young minds. Instead:

> To ask, to guess, to know, as they commence,
> As Fancy opens the quick springs of Sense,
> We ply the Memory, we load the brain,
> Bind rebel Wit, and double chain on chain . . .
> Whate'er the talents, or howe'er design'd,
> We hang one jingling padlock on the mind.
>
> (IV 155–62)

The faults Pope is ascribing to the dunces in this passage were of
a kind, of course, to which rhetoric traditionally was prone: the
same errors attributed by previous humanists to their opponents
are here attributed by Pope to the dunces. One may not accept
Pope's notion of a special or accelerated assault of duncical
rhetoric in his own time, but one can still appreciate the validity
of his concern for a certain rhetorical ideal.

In attempting to set words apart from thought, the 'schoolmaster' violates the traditional humanist view that they are
hardly separable, or at least that their rupture is pernicious in
the extreme.[2] As Thomas Sheridan, a god-son of Swift and the
father of Richard Brinsley Sheridan, says in the mid-eighteenth
century, there is 'such an intimate connection between ideas and
words, language and knowledge, that whatever deficiency, or
fault, there may be in the one, necessarily affects the other . . .
[May not the] corruptions of our understandings [be owing] to
those of our style? Are not our minds chiefly stored with ideas by
words, and must not clearness or obscurity in the one, necessarily
produce the same in the other?'[3] Here is the justification, if any

---

1. S. S. Laurie, *Studies in the History of Educational Opinion from the Renaissance* (Cambridge, Cambridge University Press, 1903), p. 63.

2. Thus Ascham, in *The Schoolmaster* (London, 1711), p. 140: 'Ye know
not, what Hurt ye do to Learning, that care not for Words, but for Matter;
and so make a Divorce betwixt the Tongue and the Heart.'

3. Sheridan, *British Education*, pp. 217, 220. Cf. the following from Ascham,
The Schoolmaster, pp. 140–1: 'whosoever be found fond in Judgment of
Matter, be commonly found as rude in uttering their Minds. . . For mark all
Ages, look upon the whole Course of both the Greek, and Latin Tongues,
and ye shall surely find, that, when apt and good Words began to be neg-
lected . . . then also began ill Deeds to spring; strange Manners to express

is needed, for Pope's use of debased verbal arts as a vehicle suggesting bigger deteriorations. A corrupt literature may be considered an index, a sign (or a metaphor, as in the *Dunciad*), pointing to more fundamental disorders. Moreover, Sheridan's view indicates the power of the word to *cause* corruption: may not obscurity in duncely writings cause Augustan minds to be darkened? May not the 'corruptions of our understandings' follow from Smithfield farces, bombastic prose, and effeminate verse? Such, at any rate, is the rationale of Pope's thesis in the *Dunciad* that a reign of literary dulness portends a cultural breakdown.

To drive a wedge between words and thought is to split, ultimately, rhetoric and philosophy, which every humanist from the time of Cicero[1] could only bewail as disastrous:

> The separation of philosophy from oratory was the main cause that both were in a short time destroyed. The union of the soul and body are [*sic*] not more necessary for any useful purpose in life, than the union of oratory and philosophy for their mutual welfare. Whilst the philosophers were busy in searching after the knowledge of things [the context seems to indicate that Sheridan in this sentence had in mind the latter part of the seventeenth century], they did not consider what an intimate connection there was between ideas and words; without a right use of which, they could neither make any sure progress themselves in science, nor justly communicate their thoughts to others.[2]

Words and things (i.e., subject matter, thought, or even, to the Royal Society and others, the physical object) had been more and more split apart during the seventeenth century. Slighting the theory that sense *informs* words, like the soul the body, the century moves from Bacon's view that 'words are but the

good Orders; new and fond Opinions to strive with old and true Doctrin, first in Philosophy, and after in Religion; right Judgment of all Things to be perverted, and so Virtue with Learning is contemned, and Study left off.'

1. Bacon (*The Advancement of Learning*, p. 129) comments on Cicero's position thus: 'So we see Cicero the orator complained of Socrates and his school, that he was the first that separated philosophy and rhetoric; whereupon rhetoric became an empty and verbal art.'

2. Sheridan, *British Education*, p. 107.

images of matter' to the Royal Society's repudiation of words in favour of things.[1] From being the means to wisdom, words become obstacles to knowledge. In the catch-phrase of the period, *res et verba*, one detects a steady shift from *res* meaning all subject matter—including the world of spirit and ideas—to *res* meaning physical thing,[2] for which *verbum* is only a label. The prestige once awarded humane letters is transferred to facts.[3] Paralleling the scientific effort to sunder *res et verba* there had been the influential attempt by Peter Ramus to reassign the first two parts of Rhetoric's traditional five-fold division—invention and disposition—to Logic, leaving to Rhetoric the duty of gilding the matter, the function of mere 'style' and delivery.[4] Such a theory (a theory of poetic ornamentation, a notion that words are clapped on to matter) undoubtedly had consequences on the level of poetic practice; it also had the effect of contributing to the separation of words and ideas that Cicero, Ascham, Sheridan—and Pope—found so baneful.

To plump for either words or things, to view utterance and thought as the objects of distinct, even incompatible, disciplines, is to bring about a schism fatal to the eloquent ideal—the man who is versed in all knowledge, and whose speech is wise with that knowledge. And the tragedy of this situation, for Pope as for Sheridan, is that the best interests of the individual, and of society, are sabotaged. Eloquence has nothing to say, wisdom cannot be communicated: the philosopher is 'wordless', the orator is 'thingless'; knowledge is divorced from practice.

1. One seventeenth-century supporter of science, William Simpson, went so far as to advocate the abandonment of all books except those which would 'communicate' experiments. See R. F. Jones, *Ancients and Moderns* (St Louis, Washington University Studies, 1936), p. 275.

2. For the history of the phrase *res et verba* in the seventeenth century, see A. C. Howell's '*Res et Verba*: Words and Things', *ELH*, 13 (1946), pp. 131–42.

3. Against the extreme view of the scientists, the Royal Society's programme of so many things in so many words, Swift reacted vigorously in *Gulliver's Travels*: 'An expedient was therefore offered, that since words are only names for *things*, it would be more convenient for all men to carry about them such *things* as were necessary to express the particular business they are to discourse on.' Not reducible to such terms, the moral and spiritual nature of man and the universe would no longer be subjects of polite conversation.

4. An account of the way Ramus 'reformed' the art of rhetoric is found in Perry Miller's *The New England Mind* (New York, The Macmillan Company, 1939). See particularly the chapter entitled 'Rhetoric'.

In the speech of the 'schoolmaster' Pope exemplifies, as William Ayre observed, 'all the Errors of common scholastick Education'.[1] Such lines as these,

> A Poet the first day, he dips his quill;
> And what the last? a very Poet still,   (IV 163–4)

certainly suggest the error of 'making all Boys make Verses, as if we were to have a Nation of Rhymers, instead of Men of good Understanding'.[2] And when the schoolmaster regrets that so many young rhymers forgo their verses for the world of politics,[3] it is evident that he has lost the ends of education in the means. The entire speech reveals clearly that oratory as practised in the Kingdom of George and Dulness is no longer to be equated with political prudence and responsibility. Men who, as orators, should uphold the 'safety . . . of the entire State'[4] are shown in the poem to be reduced to wordy servitude, in school first, in the Royal Council later. This is all that Dulness can possibly desire:

> Oh (cry'd the Goddess) for some pedant Reign!
> Some gentle James, to bless the land again;
> To stick the Doctor's Chair into the Throne,
> Give law to Words, or war with Words alone,
> Senates and Courts with Greek and Latin rule,
> And turn the Council to a Grammar School!
> For sure, if Dulness sees a grateful Day,
> 'Tis in the shade of Arbitrary Sway.
> O! if my sons may learn one earthly thing,
> Teach but that one, sufficient for a King;
> That which my Priests, and mine alone, maintain,
> Which as it dies, or lives, we fall, or reign:
> May you, may Cam, and Isis preach it long!
> "The Right Divine of Kings to govern wrong."
>   (IV 175–88)

No Augustan tires of pointing out that under tyranny oratory

---

1. *Memoirs of the Life and Writings of Alexander Pope*, II, p. 236.   2. Ibid.
3. As in lines 165 ff.:
> Pity! the charm works only in our wall,
> Lost, lost too soon in yonder House or Hall.
> There truant Wyndham ev'ry Muse gave o'er,
> There Talbot sunk, and was a Wit no more . . .
4. *de Oratore*, I viii.

cannot flourish. Writings of the age continually refer to the
decline of oratory and the arts upon the fall of popular government in Greece and Rome—with analogies drawn carefully between those times and contemporary England.[1] No doubt the
analogy particularly served Tory interests, hinting the decline of
British liberty under Walpole and the Georges, but Whigs cited
the connection too. Of the relevance of this notion to the 'schoolmaster's speech', and to Dulness's desire for 'Arbitrary Sway',
Pope's notes leave little question:

> The matter under debate is how to confine men to Words for
> life. The instructors of youth shew how well they do their
> parts; but complain that when men come into the world they
> are apt to forget their Learning, and turn themselves to useful
> Knowledge. This was an evil that wanted to be redressed.
> And this the Goddess assures them will need a more extensive
> Tyranny than that of the Grammar schools. She therefore
> points out to them the remedy, in her wishes for *arbitrary Power*;
> whose interest it being to keep men from the study of *things*,
> will encourage the propagation of *words* and *sounds*; and to
> make all sure, she wishes for another *Pedant Monarch*. . .
> Nothing can be juster than the observation here insinuated,
> that no branch of Learning thrives well under Arbitrary
> government but *Verbal*.[2]

What gives Pope's protest special pertinency is the fact that,
as rhetoric under the Roman tyrannies consisted largely in the
epideictic variety (the rhetoric most akin to flattery), so under
the Georges, it seemed to many in the age, there had come into
existence a poetic and rhetoric of duncery: adulatory birthday
odes to the king, flattering epistles to party leaders, hireling
pamphlets, government gazettes, all the literary charms able to
make 'the Venal quiet, and intrance the Dull'.[3] Doubtless Pope
and many others exaggerated the increase in their own time of
such an obsequious rhetoric; the preceding age of Dryden certainly reveals an equal capacity for irresponsible adulation. But
as a satirist Pope could not afford the relativism of a certain

1. The source most often cited by Augustan writers is of course the forty-
fourth chapter of Longinus' *On the Sublime*.
2. Note to IV 175.   3. IV 624.

judicious historical point of view. It seemed to him that the 'word' had become a general anaesthetic: its power was being used to 'bring to one dead level ev'ry mind';[1] the sovereign dulness of the age had made Englishmen

> First slave to Words, then vassal to a Name,
> Then dupe to Party; child and man the same.
>
> (IV 501–2)

But the crowning irony, perhaps, occurs with the desire of Dulness for some 'pedant Reign' in which a British sovereign would 'Give law to Words, or war with Words alone'. The sovereign, whose 'word' should order the state, as God ordered Chaos,[2] is here reduced to a royal pedagogue, and the ideal of the learned prince evaporates. The arts of eloquence and civil prudence are thwarted of their function, for the head of the state, who should combine them for the wise rule of his people, is seen as having lost the object of the one (good government) through the perversion of the other (oratory become pedantry). Corrupted by a controlled press, debased by literary hacks, and frittered away in high places, language (the 'instrument of human society'[3]) is finally seen to impose a new tyranny over the minds of men.

Having shown how the dunces devitalize the rhetorical plenum in the public schools, Pope turns to the universities in the next episode, and explores further the consequences of divorce between words and things. For this separation, as Pope's note emphasizes, is clearly the fundamental issue in Bentley's long harangue:

> Hitherto Aristarchus hath displayed the art of teaching his Pupils words, without things. He shews greater skill in what follows, which is to teach things, without profit. For with the *better sort of fool* the first expedient is, ver. 254 to 258, to run him so swiftly through the circle of the Sciences that he shall

1. IV 268.

2. That the state is sustained by the Logos is a conception going back to the Stoics. See E. V. Arnold, *Roman Stoicism* (Cambridge, Cambridge University Press, 1911), p. 275. Cf. these lines from Dryden's Epilogue to *Albion and Albanius* (the 'word' of the first line is that of James II):
> Thus Britain's basis on a word is laid,
> As by a word the world itself was made.

3. Vives, *On Education*, p. 91.

stick at nothing, nor nothing stick with him; and though some little, both of words and things, should by chance be gathered up in his passage, yet he shews, ver. 255 to 260, that it is never more of the one than just to enable him to *persecute with Rhyme*, or of the other than to *plague with Dispute*.[1]

In the study of things the student is furnished with 'what he cannot use'; in the study of words, he is 'wed to what he must divorce, a Muse'.[2] In grammatical controversy, Bentley boasts, 'on Words is still our whole debate',[3] and in philosophy a purposeless pursuit of 'useless or pernicious'[4] knowledge is encouraged:

> Full in the midst of Euclid dip at once,
> And petrify a Genius to a Dunce:
> Or set on Metaphysic ground to prance,
> Show all his paces, not a step advance. (IV 263–6)

Since a segregation of words and things is really a first step toward specialization, it is not surprising that Bentley's speech reveals an intense interest in only a part (the *minutiae*) of the whole of human experience—and thus violates the humanist ideal of encyclopaedic learning. The 'awful Aristarch's' habit—and boast—of spending his time in

> Disputes of *Me* or *Te*, of *aut* or *at*,
> To sound or sink in *cano*, O or A
> Or give up Cicero to C or K, (IV 220–2)

would have been regarded, however mistakenly, by many in the age as an activity that tended, in Bolingbroke's words, 'neither directly nor indirectly to make us better men and better citizens', and one that was 'at best but a specious and ingenious sort of idleness . . . a creditable sort of ignorance, nothing more'.[5]

The traditional conception of the grammarian apparently had included two main functions: the explication and evaluation of the text and application of it to the manners of men, and also the formal investigation of language, syntax, and related matters. The first function had been generally considered the

1. Note to IV 255. 2. IV 261–2. 3. IV 219. 4. Note to IV 255.
5. Bolingbroke, *Works* (London, 1809), III, pp. 322–3, testifies thus concerning grammatical research.

I

higher, and to it the title of 'criticism' seems to have been
reserved.[1] Pope's notes to his edition of Homer would appear to
some in the age to be in accord, presumably, with this first and
higher order of criticism,[2] while the efforts of Bentley,[3] Theobald, Scriblerus, and others, would appear as a peculiarly dis-
putatious form of the second, as the exercise of a type of 'dialectic'; a poetic crux is made the subject of a logical dispute, the
grammarians involved become as contentious as any schoolmen.
And the grammatical critics, however great their local contributions, could be said, from one point of view, to have insisted
on particulars while ignoring wholes. From this there resulted
the specialization and, what was regarded as its natural accom-
paniment, the pride,[4] which marked the pedant, against whom
Charron declares 'I denounce formal War in my Book, as looking upon them to be irreconcilable Enemies to Wisdom'.[5]

1. For some discussion of the terms see J. E. Sandys, *A History of Classical
Scholarship*, 3rd edn (Cambridge, Cambridge University Press, 1921),
I, pp. 6–11. Cf. this statement by Thomas Baker, *Reflections Upon Learning*,
7th edn (London, 1738), p. 227: 'our Modern Critics have usually . . .
degenerated into Grammarians.'

2. Cf. George Turnbull's *Observations Upon Liberal Education* (London,
1742), pp. 436–7: 'we have a commentary upon one of them (Homer, to
wit) in our own language, which shews what criticism should propose and
do, and what commentators and masters ought to aim at in their lessons
upon such classics: I mean Mr. Pope's notes added to his admirable translation of Homer. He who hath read Homer with this help . . . is indeed
capable of entering into the spirit of any author, or of *comprehending any thing
relating to human life and manners*, or the design and rules of the highest kind of
poetry. It could hardly be said before the English readers were obliged with
this commentary on Homer, that we had any thing in any language upon
any Greek or Latin authors, upon any poet at least, that answered the ends
of true criticism, or that it was not really dangerous to put into the hands of
youth, for fear of giving them the very worst of turns, a propension towards
mere verbal criticism, which, if it be not pedantry, false erudition, vain
puffing up science, what can be so called?' Italics mine.

3. Spingarn points out that Bentley dismissed with 'disdain the whole
question of the artistic quality of the Phalaris letters', and quotes him as
saying: 'What force of wit and spirit in the style, what lively painting of
humour, some fancy they discern there, I will not examine nor dispute.'
Critical Essays of the Seventeenth Century, I lxxxviii, and note.

4. Wotton and others thought the triumphs of the grammarians surpassed
the works commented on, and that there was 'required more Fineness of
Thought, and Happiness of Invention, than perhaps, Twenty such Volumes
as those were, upon which these very Criticisms were made'. See *Reflections
Upon Ancient and Modern Learning*, 3rd edn (London, 1705), pp. 359 ff.

5. Charron, *Of Wisdom*, I C^r.

Pride, specialization, idolatry of 'details' and 'facts', all these are summed up in the poet's portrait of Bentley. The great scholar disdains to vail his hat, takes pride in having humbled Milton and Horace, esteems himself superior to ancient grammarians:

> "Mistress! dismiss that rabble from your throne:
> Avaunt—is Aristarchus yet unknown?
> Thy mighty Scholiast, whose unweary'd pains
> Made Horace dull, and humbled Milton's strains.
> Turn what they will to Verse, their toil is vain,
> Critics like me shall make it Prose again.
> Roman and Greek Grammarians! know your Better:
> Author of something yet more great than Letter;
> While tow'ring o'er your Alphabet, like Saul,
> Stands our Digamma, and o'er-tops them all."
>
> (IV 209–18)

And then in language which hints at the invasion of the moral sphere by the relatively new scientific attitude, the verse goes on to say that, like a scholarly machine,

> The critic Eye, that microscope of Wit,
> Sees hairs and pores, examines bit by bit.

What the new specialist and his mechanized perceptions cannot reveal, according to Pope, is

> How parts relate to parts, or they to whole,
> The body's harmony, the beaming soul.

The proper study of mankind—the whole man, bodily harmony and beaming soul—will be seen by such a 'critic Eye' only, as Bentley says, when 'Man's whole frame is obvious to a Flea' (IV 238).

Bentley's account of the educational process by which the young nobility, 'bounded by Nature', are 'narrow'd still by Art',[1] is rudely interrupted by the noisy entry of the young fop returned from the Grand Tour, an episode that mutilates, as Maynard Mack has pointed out, 'a classical and Renaissance ideal ... of wisdom ripened by commerce with men and cities'.[2]

1. IV 503.   2. *Pope and His Contemporaries*, p. 38.

The basic metaphor of the situation, the comparison of the
young traveller to an Aeneas or Ulysses, is traditional, and was
calculated to suggest to Pope's readers a further collapse of the
humanist ideal. Ascham and George Turnbull both thus urge
the youthful tourist to model his conduct on that of the wisest of
voyagers, Ulysses,[1] and like him to become 'skilful in many
Mens Manners and Fashions', 'wise in all Purposes, and wary in
all Places'. The comparison extends even to the divinities attendant on the travellers: as Pallas (Wisdom) preserved Ulysses, so
Dulness preserves the young fop. With her

> kind cloud o'ercast,
> Safe and unseen the young Æneas past—
>
> (IV 289–90)

studying 'Mens Manners and Fashions' in a rather special
sense:

> Led by my hand, he saunter'd Europe round,
> And gather'd ev'ry Vice on Christian ground;
> Saw ev'ry Court, heard ev'ry King declare
> His royal Sense, of Op'ra's or the Fair;
> The Stews and Palace equally explor'd,
> Intrigu'd with glory, and with spirit whor'd.
>
> (IV 311–16)

It is the complete repudiation of the whole rhetorical ideal,
however, that this episode ultimately suggests. The governor of
the young fop is called, pointedly, an 'attendant Orator',[2] one
under whom his pupil

1. Pope uses Aeneas rather than Ulysses, but a comparison of the verses
describing the fop's travels (ll. 301 ff.) with this passage from Ascham (*The
Schoolmaster*, p. 71) will indicate the poet's use of the traditional relationship:
'he [the student] shall not always in his Absence out of *England*, light upon
a gentle *Alcinous*, and walk in his fair Gardens full of all harmless Pleasures;
but he shall sometimes fall either into the Hands of some cruel *Cyclops*, or into
the Lap of some wanton and dallying Dame, *Calypso*; and so suffer the
Danger of many a deadly Den, not so full of Perils to destroy the Body, as
full of vain Pleasures to poison the Mind. Some *Siren* shall sing him a Song,
sweet in Tune, but sounding in the End to his utter Destruction. If *Scylla*
drown him not, *Charybdis* may fortune to swallow him. Some *Circe* shall make
of him, of a plaine English Man, a right Italian.' In Turnbull's *Observations
Upon Liberal Education*, pp. 462–3, the relationship is again made, and the
author cites Horace as precedent. Horace's Epistle II, Book I, may be the
source of the traditional analogy.

2. IV 281.

> Dropt the dull lumber of the Latin store,
> Spoil'd his own language, and acquir'd no more;
> All Classic learning lost on Classic ground;
> And last turn'd *Air*, the Echo of a Sound! (IV 319–22)

His rhetorical training having dwindled to 'nothing but a Solo in his head', the fop, with a whore for company, returns home to prop the throne of Dulness:

> See now, half-cur'd, and perfectly well-bred . . .
> As much Estate, and Principle, and Wit,
> As Jansen, Fleetwood, Cibber shall think fit;
> Stol'n from a Duel, follow'd by a Nun,
> And, if a Borough chuse him, not undone;
> See, to my country happy I restore
> This glorious Youth, and add one Venus more.
> Her too receive (for her my soul adores)
> So may the sons of sons of sons of whores,
> Prop thine, O Empress! like each neighbour Throne,
> And make a long Posterity thy own.   (IV 323–34)

Pope is steadily asserting in Book IV the inseparable connection that the humanists believed existed between virtue and learning (a 'learning' largely acquired through the medium of the 'word'), but asserting it, of course, in reverse terms. As the 'word' gives way to meaningless sound, Wisdom is displaced by Dulness, by vice and folly. The poet's thesis is at bottom the same as Ascham's: when 'good Words began to be neglected . . . then also began ill Deeds to spring . . . new and fond Opinions to strive with old and true Doctrine . . . right Judgment of all Things to be perverted, and so Virtue with Learning is contemned, and Study left off.'

III

In its overall structure Book IV expounds, in poetic terms, the humanist position that the segregation of words and things is fatal. Almost exactly half of the book (the first 336 of a total of 656 lines) is devoted to attempts by the dunces to exist in a merely verbal or else a merely phonetic world. Here the episodes are those of Opera (to which Pope and others objected because it seemed to them to be sound without sense, and also because it appealed, in its emphasis on the spectacular, to the eye rather than to the mind); of the dunces who preach 'the Word without a call', and have the 'cant of Wit, Without the soul'; of the schoolmaster who teaches 'Words alone' and the 'Aristarch' of the universities who declares 'on Words is still our whole debate'; and, finally, of the young fop who returns 'with nothing but a Solo in his head'. 'Things' are touched upon only sketchily (for the space of twelve lines, 255–66). In this first half of the book the poet tries to show what a misconception and misuse of the 'word' leads to—debased art, 'minute critics', empty-headed wits, political vassalage, debauchery of private virtue.

In the latter half of Book IV, on the other hand, Pope is concerned with the perverted and irrational employment of 'things'. After the episode of the Grand Tour the satire revolves around the 'thingful' preoccupations of coin collectors, virtuosi, and speculative reasoners. And through the activities of such personages Pope suggests that an exclusive concern with 'things' leads to irreligion and profaneness, to a despiritualized universe, to a nation of irreverent dilettantes, godless naturalists, philosophic sceptics.

A hint of irreligion appears accordingly in the first portrait following the fop's reception. Annius, the rascally dealer in antique coinage, prays to Dulness as follows:

> Grant, gracious Goddess! grant me still to cheat,
> O may thy cloud still cover the deceit!
> Thy choicer mists on this assembly shed,
> But pour them thickest on the noble head.
> So shall each youth, assisted by our eyes,
> See other Caesars, other Homers rise;
> Thro' twilight ages hunt th' Athenian fowl,
> Which Chalcis Gods, and mortals call an Owl,
> Now see an Attys, now a Cecrops clear,
> Nay, Mahomet! the Pigeon at thine ear;
> Be rich in ancient brass, tho' not in gold,
> And keep his Lares, tho' his house be sold;
> To headless Phoebe his fair bride postpone,
> Honour a Syrian Prince above his own.   (IV 355–68)

Annius desires the nobility to forgo all natural duties in favour of what amounts (as Pope phrases it) to a species of idolatry. The wife is slighted for a 'headless Phoebe', the real Lares (all the natural pieties of an ancient English 'house' and household) are lost in the preservation of some spurious material relics of antiquity. And in the succeeding lines (where Annius is said by Mummius to have swallowed certain coins to prevent their confiscation) sacrilege plays still more strongly about the verse:

> Then taught by Hermes, and divinely bold,
> Down his own throat he risqu'd the Grecian gold;
> Receiv'd each Demi-God, with pious care,
> Deep in his Entrails—I rever'd them there,
> I bought them, shrouded in that living shrine,
> And, at their second birth, they issue mine. (IV 381–6)

In the era of George and Dulness gold is apotheosized: in the general displacement of values there is given to Caesar, imaged on the coins, the worship due to God; the 'thing', the physical object, is deified.

In any event, Pope suggests that 'Gold is the God of the Nation',[1] striking again at commercial values and at the relatively new phenomenon of finance capitalism which threatened traditional Christian attitudes toward usury and money. Under George and Dulness, we are led to believe, has begun indeed an age of gold, of golden chains and golden standards: in the realm of duncery a 'Midas sits Lord Chancellor of Plays', and Dulness is 'of Bus'ness the directing Soul'.[2] And involved in the new materialism, its logical outcome, is a turning away from God. Gold is divinized, and, like Annius, men are now 'faithful' to Mammon.

Immediately following the episode of the coin-collectors, the virtuosi, 'thick as Locusts black'ning all the ground', sweep in. The comparison suggests, as Pope indicates in a note to the line,

1. The phrase is Edward Ward's, from a poem called 'Truth without Dissembling', in *A Collection of Historical and State Poems . . . Being the Fifth Volume of Miscellanies* (London, 1717), p. 38.
2. For these examples and further discussion of Pope's concern with a commercialized society, see Hugo M. Reichard's essay, 'Pope's Social Satire: Belles-Lettres and Business', *PMLA*, 67 (1952), pp. 420–34.

that the virtuosi have lost their human qualities in a kind of metamorphosis. This extinction of man's reasonable soul is imaginatively suggested throughout the poem by other images of animal life. The dunces have taken the image of the nature they increasingly appear to idolize: some of them come 'whip and spur . . . on German Crouzaz, and Dutch Burgersdyck', others 'turn off to roll with Hogs, / To run with Horses, or to hunt with Dogs'. Annius, like the 'wily Fox is seen to creep', and Mummius 'Fierce as a startled Adder, swell'd'.

The whole character of the virtuoso episode makes clear what was wrong, in the Augustan sense, with 'virtuosity'. There was much more at stake than a joke against 'cockle-shellship'. Nature being one of the two books of Revelation God had provided for man,[1] in which man could find his true position and purpose in the total scheme of things, and by which he could ultimately attain salvation, the practice of the virtuosi, like that of the coin collectors, came very near to blasphemy. For the tendency of the virtuoso mind, as Pope saw it, was to stop with Nature itself, to be curious about How and forgetful of Why. Thus in his portraits of the florist and the entomologist Pope deplores a kind of activity which begins, and ends, with the creature, the thing;[2] the two virtuosi are made to participate in a highly blasphemous colloquy.[3] The florist mistakes Nature's ministrations to the flower he prizes so highly as his own; his words insinuate that he, not Nature, has 'suckled, and chear'd, with air, and sun, and show'r', and that he has thus engendered a blossom surpassing Nature's power:

1. See, for example, p. 43 of St Augustine's *On the Trinity* (trans. by A. W. Hadden) in vol. VII of *The Works of Aurelius Augustine*, ed. Marcus Dods (Edinburgh, 1871–7).

2. Cf. Pope's note to IV 471: 'Those who, from the effects in this Visible world, deduce the Eternal Power and Godhead of the First Cause tho' they cannot attain to an adequate idea of the Deity, yet discover so much of him, as enables them to see the End of their Creation, and the Means of their Happiness'.

Turnbull (*Observations Upon Liberal Education*, p. 132) says that natural philosophy, 'if not employed to lead youth to a just notion of the perfections of the one Lord of the universe, and of our duties resulting from thence, falls far short of its best aim and noblest use, and is indeed little better than what is justly called in contempt cockle-shellship'.

3. See the whole episode, IV 403–36.

> Did Nature's pencil ever blend such rays,
> Such vary'd light in one promiscuous blaze?
>
> (IV 411–12)

In an excess of passionate attachment he 'thrones' the creature in glass and gives it the kind of adoration due to its Creator. His complaint against the entomologist who violates his blossom in order to capture a butterfly introduces, at the same time, the theme of a rape of nature—though he fails to realize that he is as guilty in this regard as the virtuoso he indicts:

> And lo the wretch! whose vile, whose insect lust
> Lay'd this gay daughter of the Spring in dust.
>
> (IV 415–16)

Then follows in a curious fusion the admiration and predatism which define the 'insect lust' of the entomologist. Spied out, like a wood nymph in her retreat, the butterfly the entomologist lusts after is ruthlessly hunted down:

> I saw, and started from its vernal bow'r
> The rising game, and chac'd from flow'r to flow'r . . .
> And where it fix'd, the beauteous bird I seiz'd.

Contemplative appreciation of nature is superseded by desire of possession: the entomologist displays, 'fair ev'n in death', the 'spoils' of his activity. An exploiter of nature, he is interested mainly in the 'naked fact', and not even in the naked fact unless it lies within his specialty:

> Rose or Carnation was below my care;
> I meddle, Goddess! only in my sphere.
>
> (IV 431–2)

Both virtuosi are made to appear as violators of God's garden. Instead of looking 'thro' Nature up to Nature's God',[1] they focus extravagantly upon nature itself and grant to the thing the devotion properly given to God. Their concentrated and specialized preoccupation with the 'thing' results, moreover, in a fatal insulation of human activities; they become sequestered in their special aberrancies: some give their exclusive attention to

1. *An Essay on Man*, IV 332.

shells, others wander off 'in a wilderness of moss' or 'waken to a Humming-bird'.

Pope emphasizes repeatedly in the latter half of Book IV the idea that an exclusive concentration on the physical world leads to the utter elimination of the supernatural from human consciousness. The dunces devote themselves to nature and thus, in a sense, divinize it. They follow Dulness's advice to

> think their Eyes
> And Reason giv'n them but to study *Flies*!
> See Nature in some partial narrow shape,
> And let the Author of the Whole escape:
> Learn but to trifle; or, who most observe,
> To wonder at their Maker, not to serve. (IV 453–8)

In *An Essay on Man*, man is oriented in and through his relation to nature; in the *Dunciad*, man so perverts or misuses nature that he attempts, through pride, to transcend his proper status, or, through a type of self-abasement, fails to live up to his 'human' condition at all.[1] Though man, at the conclusion of *An Essay on Man*, is turned toward Heaven, which 'beholds its image in his breast', what we find in *Dunciad* IV is the dunce with a 'head that turns at super-lunar things',[2] or the virtuoso who finds 'Congenial matter in the Cockle-kind'.[3] Crouched over his cockle, man becomes subdued to the 'matter' that he works in.

The perversions of the dunces in the realm of nature lead inevitably to theological perversions, and so Pope introduces at this point a 'gloomy Clerk',

> Sworn foe to Myst'ry,[4] yet divinely dark;
> Whose pious hope aspires to see the day
> When Moral Evidence shall quite decay.

(IV 460–2)

1. 'There are indeed some Studies, wherein a Scrutinous Curiosity is altogether impertinent and ridiculous; as when we would busie our Thoughts about things that can neither reform our Morals, nor enlighten our Understandings, when we either sink them to mean and frivolous Niceties, or raise them to secret unknowable Disquisitions. And yet these two extreams have strangely engaged many great Men'. Thomas Rymer (?), *An Essay, Concerning Critical and Curious Learning* (London, 1698), pp. 5–6.

2. *Dunciad*, IV 451. The line refers to speculations concerning the possibility of flights to the moon. Cf. note to IV 452.

3. IV 448.   4. 'Mystery' in the sense of divine revelation.

The Clerk expounds the origin of duncery in Pride. Dulness, he says, is the Goddess of Pride:

> All-seeing in thy mists, we want no guide,
> Mother of Arrogance, and Source of Pride!

In the service of Pride the dunces

> Make God Man's Image, Man the final Cause . . .[1]
> See all in *Self*, and but for self be born:
> Of nought so certain as our *Reason* still,
> Of nought so doubtful as of *Soul* and *Will*.
>
> (IV 478, 480–2)

The humanist view was that contemplation of the creation should lead to humility; man first had to learn his relative insignificance in the total plan so that, through a humble approach toward the creation, his rehabilitation could be effected within its proper limits (this is the progress of events in *An Essay on Man*).[2] Preoccupied with *minutiae*, with the part, the dunces never acquire such a perspective on man, never see the 'relative' insignificance of their position. They are thus led to pride; their activity may lead to the 'measuring', as Pope says, of God's 'Attributes by ours', even, perhaps, to a removal of God from the universe altogether. The last of these errors was exemplified for the age, of course, by Descartes. With Descartes came in the threat of a mechanical universe no longer in need of a God when set in motion; a universe in which we

> shove him off as far as e'er we can;
> Thrust some Mechanic Cause into his place.

Throughout the last half of Book IV 'Nature', as Pope says, is

1. Cf. Charron, *Of Wisdom*, II, p. 761: 'most other Errors and Defects in Religion, are owing chiefly to Want of right and becoming Apprehensions of God. We debase and bring him down to us, compare and judge him by our selves, cloath him with our Infirmities and unaccountable Humours, and then proportion and suit our Worship and Services accordingly'.

2. Ibid., p. 766: 'Religion consists in the Knowledge of God, and of our Selves. For this is a relative Duty, and these are the two Terms of that Relation. Its Business is to magnify God, and set him as high, and to humble Man and lay him as low, as possibly we can. To subdue and beat him down, as a lost worthless Wretch; and when this is once done, then to furnish him with Helps and Means of raising himself up again'.

made to 'still encroach upon [God's] plan'.[1] And this new
naturalism is confirmed in the person of Dulness: all the naturalistic suggestions of the poem finally are concentrated in the Goddess herself, and she begins to appear as a nature deity, as that
nature which the dunces, in manifold ways, have divinized.
This idolatry of the thing, this divinization of nature itself, is
heartily advocated by the Clerk:

> Oh hide the God still more! and make us see
> Such as Lucretius drew, a God like Thee:
> Wrapt up in Self, a God without a Thought,
> Regardless of our merit or default.
> Or that bright Image to our fancy draw,
> Which Theocles in raptur'd vision saw,
> While thro' Poetic scenes the Genius roves,
> Or wanders wild in Academic Groves;
> That Nature our Society adores,
> Where Tindal dictates, and Silenus snores.
>
>   (IV 483–92)

The passage is a criticism of a mélange of naturalistic, panthe-
istic, and epicurean notions, notions that were to become increasingly fashionable in the centuries following Pope. Faced
with a Nature from which the Divine Intelligence, the $No\hat{u}s$ as
Pope says,[2] had been abstracted, man is shown as having lost his
traditional orientation, and as having suffered a loss with respect to function and purpose. His only resource, perhaps, was
the 'raptur'd vision' of a Shaftesbury—or, in the times to come,
of a Wordsworth.

1. IV 473.
2. Cf. the earlier line, 'And much Divinity without a $No\hat{u}s$' (IV 244), and
Pope's comment upon it: '$No\hat{u}s$ was the Platonic term for *Mind*, or the *first
Cause*, and that system of Divinity is here hinted at which terminates in blind
Nature without a $No\hat{u}s$: such as the Poet afterward describes' at ll. 485 ff.

THE ANTI-CHRIST OF WIT

I

WITH the exception of the *Aeneid*, no poem 'enters' into Pope's world of duncery more than *Paradise Lost*.[1] In a sense the poet's imitations of Milton (imitations which range from overt allusion to the barest hint) can be said to form one dimension of the *Dunciad*'s meaning. From Pope's parodying of Milton results a tacit suggestion that the *Dunciad*, like *Paradise Lost*, is about a war between good and evil. Milton's devils appear to revive in a new context, there to prosper so well —as dunces—that they carry to conclusion the work of destruction introduced by Satan: the *Dunciad* ends when the 'dread Empire' of Chaos is 'restored'.

This orientation for duncery is evinced in Pope's selection of most of his Miltonic materials from satanic contexts, a principle of selection which seems to have gone unnoticed by those critics and editors who over the years have recognized one or another isolated instance of Pope's parodying.[2] The Devil, Sin, and Death, along with the entire host of rebel angels, are drawn into the action of the *Dunciad* and are made to impart some of their infernality to the dunces. The world of dulness is infiltrated by powers of darkness, so that the comedy is constantly jostled by more serious implications. Although the Miltonic influence may often appear to be no more than a shading in the language, the shading is significant; and the frequency of overt imitation (Pope noted many of the parallels himself) gives a directional value to the verse in which even the slighter allusions soon participate.

The satanic light projected upon the dunces is strikingly ex-

1. I have not made an actual count of the imitations, but a glance at the index in the *Twick. Ed.* will confirm this view. There are, in addition, many echoes of *Paradise Lost* unnoted by editors.
2. Even those few parodies unrelated to the rebel angels are usually used to connect the dunces with a kind of impiety. See the butterfly fancier's speech, *Twick. Ed.*, p. 383 (ll. 427–8, and note).

emplified at the opening of Book II, where Colley Cibber (who in 1743 replaced Theobald as King of the Dunces) and all his cohorts are transformed by it into forces of anti-Christ:

> High on a gorgeous seat, that far out-shone
> Henley's gilt Tub, or Fleckno's Irish Throne,
> Or that where on her Curls the Public pours,
> All-bounteous, fragrant Grains and Golden show'rs,
> Great Cibber sate:[1] The proud Parnassian sneer,
> The conscious simper, and the jealous leer,
> Mix on his look: All eyes direct their rays
> On him, and crowds turn Coxcombs as they gaze.
> His Peers shine round him with reflected grace,
> New edge their dulness, and new bronze their face.
> So from the Sun's broad beam, in shallow urns
> Heav'ns twinkling Sparks draw light, and point their
>   horns.[2]
>   Not with more glee, by hands Pontific crown'd,
> With scarlet hats wide-waving circled round,
> Rome in her Capitol saw Querno sit,
> Thron'd on sev'n hills, the Antichrist of wit.

Even the movement of the verse becomes Miltonic here, as Warton noted,[3] bringing a vision of a new kind of Hell raised in the midst of Augustan London—a *Panmoronium* that we cannot contemplate to the exclusion of its great original. And while there is designed absurdity in comparing Colley Cibber, the

1. Pope notes the source, *P.L.*, II 1–5:
>   High on a Throne of Royal State, which far
>   Outshon the wealth of *Ormus* and of *Ind,*
>   Or where the gorgeous East with richest hand
>   Showrs on her Kings *Barbaric* Pearl & Gold,
>   Satan exalted sat . . .
2. Gilbert Wakefield, *Observations on Pope* (London, 1796), pp. 298–9, noted the parallel to *P.L.*, VII 364–6:
>   Hither as to thir Fountain other Starrs
>   Repairing, in their gold'n Urns draw Light,
>   And hence the Morning Planet guilds his horns.
3. Warton's edition of Pope's *Works* (London, 1798), v, p. 126. Warton noted that the lines in the passage 'run more into one another, than in any other part of our author's works'. Harte, in his *An Essay on Satire*, made this comment:
>   See Querno's Throne, by hands Pontific rise,
>   And a Fool's Pandaemonium strike our Eyes!

anti-Christ of wit, with a far more awesome anti-Christ, Satan, there filters through the comic glaze the suggestion that even the shallowest urn may hold a formidable amount of unholy power. In short, what the Miltonic resources enable the poet to do, though humorously, is to shadow forth, in metaphor, the implicit evil in duncery, and to associate the dulness of his poem with the diabolism of *Paradise Lost*.

This association pervades the *Dunciad* everywhere. In Book IV, for instance, the satanic potentates, having assumed (as spirits can) a duncely shape, are gathered as in the infernal conclave of Pandaemonium. First Moloch, now in the guise of a master of public schools:

> lo! a Spectre rose, whose index-hand
> Held forth the Virtue of the dreadful wand;
> His beaver'd brow a birchen garland wears,
> Dropping with Infant's blood, and Mother's tears.[1]
> (IV 139–42)

Then Beëlzebub, in the shape of Bentley:

> Before them march'd that awful Aristarch;
> Plow'd was his front with many a deep Remark.[2]
> (IV 203–4)

Earlier in the poem the lesser orders[3] of dunces and of devils have also been brought into metaphoric fellowship. The number

1. Warburton noted the source (*P.L.*, I 392–3):
> First *Moloch*, horrid King besmear'd with blood
> Of human sacrifice, and parents tears.
2. The verse really recalls two Miltonic figures: Beëlzebub, who at the hellish council (*P.L.*, II 301–3):
> rose and in his rising seem'd
> A Pillar of State; deep on his Front engraven
> Deliberation sat and public care;
and Satan:
> yet shon
> Above them all th' Arch Angel: but his face
> Deep scars of Thunder had intrench . . .
> (*P.L.*, I 599–601)
3. There are other instances of individual caricatures. For example, this line,
> Rowz'd by the light, old Dulness heav'd the head, (I 257 B)
recalls Satan, who never 'Had ris'n or heav'd his head' off the burning lake if God had not so permitted. Cf. *P.L.*, I 209–11. Cf. also the parodies of Satan, below.

of the dunces is as the number of the fiends: their common home
is the north, the seat of evil; their onslaught is annihilative,
barbarous:

> Soon as they dawn, from Hyperborean skies
> Embody'd dark, what clouds of Vandals rise!
> Lo! where Maeotis sleeps, and hardly flows
> The freezing Tanais thro' a waste of snows,
> The North by myriads pours her mighty sons,
> Great nurse of Goths, of Alans, and of Huns![1]
>
> (III 85–90 B)

The souls of unborn dunces are like the assembling hosts of
Satan, endless reserves in the battle against God:

> Millions and millions on these banks he views,
> Thick as the stars of night, or morning dews.[2]

The encounter of the impresarios of the theatres is like the
shadowy encounter of the monster Death with Satan in Book II
of *Paradise Lost*:

> But lo! to dark encounter in mid air
> New wizards rise; I see my Cibber there!

1. As Courthope noted, the lines parallel Milton's simile (*P.L.*, I 351–4)
describing the devils as
> A multitude, like which the populous North
> Pour'd never from her frozen loyns, to pass
> *Rhen* or *Danaw*, when her barbarous Sons
> Came like a Deluge on the South.

Medieval dialecticians were traditionally termed (by Petrarch and Erasmus)
the Goths and Huns of learning, and thus Pope's simile hints at the quarrel
between the humanists and the schoolmen discussed in the last chapter.
See Marshall McLuhan, 'An Ancient Quarrel in Modern America', *The
Classical Journal*, 41 (1946), p. 159.

2. Here are the apostate angels (*P.L.*, V 743–6):
> Satan with his Powers
> Far was advanc't on winged speed, an Host
> Innumerable as the Starrs of Night,
> Or Starrs of Morning, Dew-drops.

Pope mentions Virgil as the source of his simile. It is true that the situation
in Pope's verse—souls awaiting birth—is more akin to that of the Virgilian
original (*Aeneid*, VI 309–11, where departed spirits are described) than to
Milton's; but Pope's debt to Milton is indicated by verbal similarities and by
the fact that Virgil compares the souls to the leaves of the forest and to the
birds that migrate, *not* to the stars of night and to morning dews. In the
notes Pope at times appears to conceal his Miltonic sources. Cf. note to l.
314 of Book II, and comment by Sutherland.

> Booth in his cloudy tabernacle shrin'd,
> On grinning dragons thou shalt mount the wind.
> Dire is the conflict, dismal is the din,
> Here shouts all Drury, there all Lincoln's-inn.
>
> (III 265–70 B)

The first line of the passage should recall Milton's description of Satan and Death as 'two black Clouds' which, in their confrontation, stand

> Hov'ring a space, till Winds the signal blow
> To joyn their dark Encounter in mid air.
>
> (*P. L.*, II 716–18)

And the last two lines of Pope's verses are, as noted before,[1] a parody of these describing war in heaven:

> dire was the noise
> Of conflict; over head the dismal hiss
> Of fiery Darts in flaming volies flew.
>
> (*P. L.*, VI 211–13)

Milton's monstrous figure of Sin, and her son Death, also make their 'presences' known in several contexts of the *Dunciad*. One such manifestation revives the moment in *Paradise Lost* when Sin proposes that they construct a bridge between Hell and Earth. Undeterred by the journey through the vast abyss, Sin says she cannot

> miss the way, so strongly drawn
> By this new felt attraction and instinct.
>
> (*P.L.*, x 262–3)

Pope, as Maynard Mack has pointed out, transfers Sin's obscene instinct to the dunces. As Sin is 'attracted' to earth by the odour of mortality, so the dunces are 'irresistibly drawn into the gravitational field of Dulness—

> "by sure Attraction led
> And strong impulsive gravity of Head." '[2]

In another instance, Cibber's wonder and awe at the vision of the future awarded him in Book III is made to match the amazement of Satan as he views the 'stupendious Bridge' created by

1. See above, p. 98.   2. *Pope and His Contemporaries*, p. 29.

Sin and Death—a collocation strengthening Pope's implication that the 'new world' is egocentric, original with the dunces and their folly:

> Joy fills his soul, joy innocent of thought;
> "What pow'r, he cries, what pow'r these wonders wrought?"
> "Son [Settle replies]; what thou seek'st is in thee."[1]

> "And are these wonders, Son, to thee unknown?
> Unknown to thee? These wonders are thy own."[2]

Here is the passage from Milton:

> Great joy was at thir meeting, and at sight
> Of that stupendious Bridge his joy encreas'd.
> Long hee admiring stood, till Sin, his faire
> Inchanting Daughter, thus the silence broke.
> O Parent, these are thy magnific deeds,
> Thy Trophies, which thou view'st as not thine own.
>
> (X 350–5)

As this last passage suggests, however, the Miltonic figure most perfectly amenable to Pope's purposes is Satan himself, the Supreme Negator and hence (in Pope's transvaluation) the Supreme Dunce.[3] The rule of Cibber, inaugurated by 'Loud thunder' that 'to its bottom shook the bog',[4] finds its counterpart in Satan's escape from Hell to the roar of

> Harsh Thunder, that the lowest bottom shook
> Of *Erebus*.[5]

Thus too, like the Great Apostate who 'at one slight bound high over leap'd all bound'[6] and proceeded to subvert Creation, the dunces,

> at one bound o'er-leaping all his laws,
> Make God Man's Image, Man the final Cause.[7]

---

1. *Dunciad*, III 249–51 B.   2. III 273–4 B.

3. If sin is rebellion against the will of an omnipotent God then it is implicitly, in one perspective, foolish, even duncical. Milton brings out this ridiculous aspect of sin when he has God laugh at Satan's presumptuous efforts against His Throne.

4. I 329 B.   5. *P.L.*, II 882–3.

6. Cf. *P.L.*, IV 180 ff., where Satan's entry into Paradise is described.

7. The dunces turn creation upside down, the universe becomes egocentric rather than theocentric. Sir Thomas Browne had described this process

In the same way, at the opening of Book IV, the 'darkness visible' of a Hell transferred to earth has overpowered the order of light and reason, and the world is ready for Chaos and old Night:

> Yet, yet a moment, one dim Ray of Light
> Indulge, dread Chaos, and eternal Night!
> Of darkness visible so much be lent,
> As half to shew, half veil the deep Intent.
> Ye Pow'rs! whose Mysteries restor'd I sing,
> To whom Time bears me on his rapid wing,
> Suspend a while your Force inertly strong,
> Then take at once the Poet and the Song.
>
> (IV 1–8)

This particular verse paragraph is a Miltonic medley: some of the references, as in l. 6, are fairly innocent,[1] but even those are woven into the larger pattern of malign suggestion—that established by 'Chaos', 'Night', 'darkness visible', and 'deep Intent'. In Book IX of *Paradise Lost* Milton uses 'intent' repeatedly in connection with Satan's purposed conquest of creation:

> I . . . thus wrapt in mist
> Of midnight vapor glide obscure, and prie
> In every Bush and Brake, where hap may finde
> The Serpent sleeping, in whose magic foulds
> To hide me, and the *dark Intent* I bring.[2]

As the *Dunciad* more and more suggests, dunce and devil, in grotesque confederacy, pursue the same 'intent'.

The common intent, of course, is the uncreating of creation, the disordering of order, and to precipitate these suggestions

---

of inversion: 'Men being unprovided, or unsufficient for higher speculations . . . will always betake themselves unto sensible representations, and can hardly be restrained the dulness of idolatry. A sin or folly not only derogatory unto God but man; overthrowing their reason as well as his divinity. In brief a reciprocation, or rather an inversion of the creation, making God one way, as he made us another; that is, after our image, as he made us after his own'. See Browne's *Works*, ed. Simon Wilkin, Bohn Library Series (London, 1852), I, p. 19.

1. For the source of the line see Milton's Sonnet Seven.

2. Cf. *P.L.*, IX 158–62. Italics mine. Other instances of the word used in the same connection are at IX 295, 462.

Pope constantly feeds into the poem, as we have seen, the
imagery of chaos—in poetry ('Figures ill pair'd, and Similes unlike'[1]), in politics ('turn the Council to a Grammar School'[2]), in
the theatre ('The forests dance, the rivers upward rise, / Whales
sport in woods, and dolphins in the skies'[3]). But most especially
it is the imagery of Milton's Chaos. There is Satan's journey
through this primeval anarchy, and Cibber's through his
thought:

> Studious he sate, with all his books around,
> Sinking from thought to thought, a vast profound!
> Plung'd for his sense, but found no bottom there;
> Then writ, and flounder'd on, in mere despair.
> He roll'd his eyes that witness'd huge dismay;[4]
>
> (I 1 1 1–15 A)

or Lintot's, in the dirtying race of publishers:

> As when a dab-chick waddles thro' the copse
> On feet and wings, and flies, and wades, and hops;
> So lab'ring on, with shoulders, hands, and head,
> Wide as a wind-mill all his figures [sic] spread,
> With arms expanded Bernard rows his state.[5]
>
> (II 63–7 B)

1. I 66 B.   2. IV 180.   3. III 245–6 B.

4. L. 115 of this passage is omitted in the 1743 texts, so I have cited the
1729 version; it parodies, as Pope noted, these lines in *P.L.*, (I 56–7),
describing Satan in torment on the burning lake:
> round he throws his baleful eyes
> That witness'd huge affliction and dismay.

In the *Satire against Mankind*, l. 18, Rochester had said that man,
> Stumbling from thought to thought, falls headlong down,

falls, that is, from the heights of vain reasoning, an appropriate context for
Pope's line. The reader should have in mind, of course, the following passage
from *P.L.*, describing Satan's progress through the void:
> thence many a League
> As in a cloudy Chair ascending rides
> Audacious, but that seat soon failing, meets
> A vast vacuitie: all unawares
> Fluttring his pennons vain plumb down he drops
> Ten thousand fadom deep.   (II 927–34)

Pope gives this note to his lines: 'The progress of a bad Poet in his thoughts
being (like the progress of the Devil in *Milton*) thro' a Chaos, might probably
suggest this imitation.'

5. Cf. *P.L.*, II 947–50, 927–8:
> So eagerly the fiend
> Ore bog or steep, through strait, rough, dense, or rare,

Moreover, and most important, there is Satan's promise to the monarchs of this wild and warring realm:

> direct my course;
> Directed, no mean recompense it brings
> To your behoof, if I that Region lost,
> All usurpation thence expell'd, reduce
> To her original darkness and your sway
> (Which is my present journey) and once more
> Erect the Standard there of *ancient Night*.
>
> (*P.L.*, II 980–6)

Pope nowhere imitates this passage locally, but it is the episode upon which the entire action of the *Dunciad* can be said to pivot. For what the *Dunciad* is 'about' is in one sense the fulfilment of Satan's vow to restore to Chaos all creation. What God had wrung from the void, Satan—and the dunces—intend to return to it. It is as if Satan and his minions, now under a comic mask, are finally able to return to Dulness, the 'Daughter of Chaos and eternal Night', her rightful dominion (by inheritance[1]) over the universe at large. This is the 'Restoration' of 'her old Empire' which marks, as Pope says, 'the Completion of the Poem',[2] and

---

> With head, hands, wings, or feet pursues his way,
> And swims or sinks, or wades, or creeps, or flyes . . .
>
> At last his Sail-broad Vannes
> He spreads for flight.

1. Here is the parentage of Dulness (I 9–18 B):
> In eldest time, e'er mortals writ or read,
> E'er Pallas issu'd from the Thund'rer's head,
> Dulness o'er all possess'd her ancient right,
> Daughter of Chaos and eternal Night:
> Fate in their dotage this fair Ideot gave,
> Gross as her sire, and as her Mother grave,
> Laborious, heavy, busy, bold, and blind,
> She rul'd, in native Anarchy, the mind.
> Still her old Empire to restore she tries,
> For, born a Goddess, Dulness never dies.

2. Near the end of the poem we behold advancing
> the sable Throne . . .
> Of *Night* Primaeval, and of *Chaos* old.

The lines should recall these from *P.L.*:
> when strait behold the Throne
> Of *Chaos*, and his dark Pavilion spread
> Wide on the wasteful Deep; with him Enthron'd
> Sat Sable-vested Night, eldest of things.   (II 959–62)

which, held in abeyance briefly by the poet's invocation at the opening of Book IV—

> Yet, yet a moment, one dim Ray of Light
> Indulge, dread Chaos, and eternal Night—

is completed in the famous close:

> Thy hand, great Anarch! lets the curtain fall;
> And Universal Darkness buries All.

Behind Pope's invocation to Chaos and Darkness at the beginning of Book IV of the *Dunciad* there stands, significantly, Milton's invocation to Light at the beginning of Book III of *Paradise Lost*. And it is in a rather special sense that Pope's forces of uncreation should be contrasted with Milton's 'bright effluence of bright essence increate'. In *Paradise Lost* Milton, drawing upon an ancient tradition which, for all practical purposes, equated light with 'being',[1] and darkness with 'non-being', speaks of the 'void profound of unessential night', meaning the realm of Chaos 'without being or substance',[2] and of the 'wide womb of uncreated night'—a night in which Satan is afraid he will lose his 'being'.[3] With the same emphasis Henry Ainsworth commented, in 1621, on the line from Genesis, 'darkness was upon the face of the deep', in these terms: 'It is not sayd God created *darknes*, for it was but the want or privation of light, and so meere nothing'.[4] When, at the end of the poem, Chaos is restored and 'Universal Darkness buries All', the poet presents us with the supreme image of 'uncreation', the reversion of the universe to the darkness of a 'void and formless infinite'. The poet replaces the light and order of the created universe with the 'non-being' which Chaos and Darkness signify. It is this wholesale annihilation of

1. In this connection see Edgar De Bruyne's *Études D'Esthétique Médiévale*, 3 vols. (Brugge, 'De Tempel', 1946), especially Chap. I of vol. III, 'L'Esthétique de la Lumière'. See also the introduction to Clare Riedl's translation of Robert Grosseteste's *De Luce* (Milwaukee, Marquette University Press, 1942). I am indebted to Mr W. K. Wimsatt for calling my attention to the tradition which equated 'light' with 'being'.

2. See Merritt Hughes' edition of *Paradise Lost* (New York, The Odyssey Press, Inc., 1935), note to II 438–9.

3. See *P.L.*, II 146–50.

4. See *Annotations Upon the first book of Moses, called Genesis* (London, 1621), A2ᵛ.

the *being* God imparted to the universe that the poet sought to convey when he said,

> Then rose the Seed of Chaos, and of Night,
> To blot out Order, and extinguish Light.
>
> (IV 13–14)

The promise of Milton's Satan to the monarch of Chaos, then, and the return to Chaos and Darkness which the *Dunciad* celebrates, are more than superficially linked. Milton and Pope are both attempting to dramatize the nature of evil, which in Christian thought aims always at the destruction of creation. Since the universe exists by virtue of the 'being' imparted to it by God, and since Chaos and Darkness represent the realm of 'non-being', this imaginative restoration is the ultimate destruction— un-creation. No other action could have better realized for Pope's readers the Christian concept of evil—that which is the annihilation and negation of the good. And by no other means could Pope have so readily revealed the evil implicit in duncery as he conceived it than by his parody of *Paradise Lost*, the metaphoric alliance of duncery with diabolism. Fashioning the *Dunciad* from whatever materials were at hand—waste paper, indigent writers, spoiled peers, cockle-shells and custard—Pope yet instils within the poem his own great argument.

II

To the final edition of the *Dunciad* Pope added two notes of particular importance. The author, he said,

> in this work had indeed a *deep Intent*; there were in it *Mysteries* or ἀπόρρητα which he durst not fully reveal, and doubtless in divers verses (according to *Milton*)
> —*more is meant than meets the ear*.[1]

And elsewhere he remarked that

> those who have the true key will find he sports with nobler quarry, and embraces a larger compass; or (as one saith, on a like occasion)

1. Note to IV 4.

> *Will see his work, like Jacob's ladder, rise,*
> *Its foot in dirt, its head amid the skies.*[1]

Into the *Dunciad* Pope artfully introduced a frame of reference kept purposely elusive, even secretive (as the above notes indicate). From some of his notes it appears that the poet is both anxious to reveal, and yet concerned to hide, the theological metaphor that gives to his subject its profoundest meaning. This coyness on Pope's part may be due to a desire to whet the reader's curiosity. In addition, a frank statement of his purposes might sound trite. But since the theotechny of the *Dunciad* involves a metaphoric inversion or reversal of a great amount of Christian theology, the poet's reticence is understandable on other grounds. He had to avoid the charge of blasphemy; he may have wished to disengage somewhat the religious metaphor from the poem's general comic foundation—to keep it clear of the broader comedy, yet evident enough to lend a graver turn to his subject. And although an effort to discuss such a metaphoric webbing as I have outlined runs the risk of stating too baldly what Pope keeps something less than overt, yet in this section I wish at least to suggest the character of the Mysteries Pope said he 'durst not fully reveal'.

Possession of what Pope means by the 'true key' to his poem depends primarily, I think, upon recognizing his thoroughgoing technique of 'inversion'. We have been concerned, in a sense, with this technique all along, mock epic consisting essentially in an inversion of epic contexts and the dunces in inversion of the epic heroes. And there is evidence to suggest that inversion was often an element in Pope's poetic practice. For example, in the unpublished Spence papers owned by Mr James Osborn there is this statement: 'Mr. Pope is now employd in a large design for a Moral Poem: there will be several Behaviors of Men flung into Fables: one in particular on the Misery of Affluence (pland just like yt of Job only wth ye Contrary point in view) . . .'[2] When Pope speaks, in *An Essay on Man*, of the

---

1. Note to I 15 B.
2. Additional Anecdotes, Box 1320, no. 7, p. 7. This statement is signed 'Col[n] Hay' (according to Mr Osborn 'Colonel Hay' is Robert Hay, 1703–56, a nephew to the second Earl of Oxford). Mr Osborn very kindly

'enormous faith' which seeks to '*invert* the world',[1] one can scarcely avoid thinking of the world that was shown as inverted in Theobald's vision near the end of Book III of the *Dunciad*. The process of inversion is continued, moreover, in the portrayal of the anti-Muses or antithetical spirits of Logic and Rhetoric near the beginning of Book IV:

> There foam'd rebellious *Logic*, gagg'd and bound,
> There, stript, fair *Rhet'ric* languish'd on the ground;
> His blunted Arms by *Sophistry* are born,
> And shameless *Billingsgate* her Robes adorn.   (23–6)

And the catastrophe of the *Dunciad* is caused of course by an anti-Logos: 'Light dies before thy uncreating word'.

Pope carries out his greatest project of inversion in the *Dunciad*, for there he constructs a negative image of Christian theology, fashioning an inverse paradigm of creation with a deity in it who parodies antithetically the Christian Deity. Opposed to the ordered 'nature' and light of a divinely sustained creation the poem offers the disnature and darkness of a 'new world' ever verging on chaos; and opposed to God it offers the goddess Dulness. The Christian positives—nature, Christ, Wisdom—are faced in the *Dunciad* with their negative inversions—disnature, anti-Christ, Dulness—as Pope seeks to convey the anti-religious values of duncery and to realize imaginatively the negativism of evil and duncery. We have already seen that, in the 1728 versions of the poem, these lines occur near the end of Book III:

> Let there be darkness! (the dread pow'r shall say)
> All shall be darkness, as it ne'er were Day.

And though this inversion of the divine fiat, presumably too clearly revelatory of Pope's 'deep Intent', disappeared after the 1728 editions, it indicates the compass of his conception of Dulness, and her capacity as an anti-Creator.

---

made portions of his collection available to me, and I wish to acknowledge my gratitude to him here. The passage quoted in my text will appear in his forthcoming edition of the Spence papers.

1. *An Essay on Man*, III 241, 243. L. 254 in the same Epistle of the *Essay*,
Saw Gods descend, and Fiends infernal rise,
should be compared with this line from Theobald's vision:
Hell rises, Heav'n descends, and dance on Earth. (III 237 B)

In the pantheon of poetry no deity has remained, perhaps, so mysterious as the goddess Dulness. In Highet's words, 'no one knows who she is meant to be'.[1] Yet some clarification of her poetic character seems possible and desirable, especially since Pope, in the last edition of the *Dunciad*, introduces a textual change and a note which place all responsibility for the work of duncery on the goddess. Instead of the previous opening,

> Books and the Man I sing, the first who brings
> The Smithfield Muses to the Ear of Kings,

the poem begins in 1743 with

> The Mighty Mother, and her Son who brings
> The Smithfield Muses to the ear of Kings.

On which Pope comments:

> The Reader ought here to be cautioned, that the *Mother*, and not the *Son*, is the principal Agent of this Poem: The latter of them is only chosen as her Collegue . . . the main action of the Poem being by no means the Coronation of the Laureate, which is performed in the very first book, but the Restoration of the Empire of Dulness in Britain, which is not accomplish'd 'till the last.[2]

In one sense the critical uncertainty about Dulness is understandable, for unlike most poetic deities she is not conceived anthropomorphically. Pope has modelled her, instead, on the Christian Supreme Being, has made her an imitation of pure being, a condition the human imagination comprehends vaguely at best. And as the human effort to realize the nature of pure being usually settles on qualities of mind, so does it, ironically, in the case of Dulness. It is her divine 'mind', a pure unthinking substance, rather than any physical shape, which oozes in grey immanence throughout the poem's world. This accounts for the vagueness of her being (a vagueness which, at the same time, reveals her 'negativism', the absence of the positive good which

---

1. *M.L.R.*, 36, p. 331.
2. This note is usually explained as an attempt to meet the charge that the hero 'does nothing'. It seems to me, however, another attempt by Pope to reveal the theological metaphor under discussion.

the concept of 'being' involves). She rules, 'in native Anarchy, the mind', she is called the 'mindful Queen', a 'Divinity without a *Noûs*', a 'God without a Thought'.[1] Dulness is essentially all 'mind' in the poem, but as these examples make clear it is the inversion of what is ordinarily thought of as the pure being of God, for whom to be is, as St Augustine says, to be wise.[2] For the creator of a world of duncery, to be is to be empty. The only real image we receive of Dulness in the poem is, furthermore, that of a being concealed, as the Christian God typically is, in darkness. Like Milton's Source of Light, who resides 'midst Thick clouds and dark' and with the 'Majesty of darkness round / Covers his Throne',[3] Pope's Source of Darkness shines, on her throne, in 'clouded Majesty', or 'A veil of fogs dilates her awful face', or, as 'She mounts the Throne: her head a Cloud'[4] conceals.

In a subtle passage near the beginning of Book I the relationship between God and Dulness is expanded. Dulness is seen introspecting a chaos out of chaos, as the Christian God, by viewing within Himself the ideal forms of all things, introspects a world. Within her 'mind' Dulness

> beholds the Chaos dark and deep,
> Where nameless Somethings in their causes sleep,
> 'Till genial Jacob, or a warm Third day,
> Call forth each mass, a Poem, or a Play:
> How hints, like spawn, scarce quick in embryo lie,
> How new-born nonsense first is taught to cry . . .
> There motley Images her fancy strike . . .[5]

1. See I 16 B, I 95 B, IV 244, IV 485.
2. See p. 184 of St Augustine's treatise *On the Trinity*, in vol. VII of *The Works of Aurelius Augustine*, ed. Marcus Dods (Edinburgh, 1871-7).
3. *P.L.*, II 263 ff.
4. See *Dunciad*, I 45 B, I 262 B, IV 17. The darkness which invests God is of course in opposition to that associated with Dulness. God, as Milton says, is 'dark with excessive bright' (*P.L.*, III 380). The darkness of Dulness is unqualified darkness, the absence or negation of all light.
5. See the whole passage, I 55-78 B. Akenside (*The Pleasures of the Imagination*, Book I 64-6) treats the same conception in these lines, somewhat more soberly than Pope:

> Then liv'd the Almighty One: then, deep-retir'd
> In his unfathom'd essence, view'd the forms,
> The forms eternal of created things.

Cf. St Thomas, *Summa Theologica*, trans. by Fathers of the English Dominican Province (New York, Benziger Brothers, Inc., 1947), First Part, ques. 44,

Like God, Dulness beholds within herself her creatures 'in their causes'. The chief difference is that the 'forms' she views are those of misformed things:[1] abortive fancies and poetic monstrosities, all the 'Grub-street-race' to which she imparts 'being' and which populates her world. A little later the resemblance to God is amplified in these lines:

> All these, and more, the cloud-compelling Queen
> Beholds thro' fogs, that magnify the scene.
> She, tinsell'd o'er in robes of varying hues,
> With self-applause her wild creation views;
> Sees momentary monsters rise and fall,
> And with her own fools-colours gilds them all.
>
> (I 79–84 B)

As God viewed His creation and saw that it was good, so Dulness, with 'self-applause', regards her 'creation'—a disnatured world of Dulness, which, in the poem, seems to have effaced, even replaced, the 'real' world, and which is filled with dunces made in her image.

That the dunces *are* made in the image of Dulness, and that we are justified in drawing the precise theological parallel, is borne out everywhere in the poem. In the following passage, which presents us with a historical, genealogical 'progress', the spirit of Dulness is seen to endure through the ages, embodied in one dull writer after another. Here are the 'chosen'[2] people:

> She [Dulness] saw, with joy, the line immortal run,
> Each sire imprest and glaring in his son:
> So watchful Bruin forms, with plastic care,
> Each growing lump, and brings it to a Bear.
> She saw old Pryn in restless Daniel shine,
> And Eusden eke out Blackmore's endless line;

---

art. 3: 'And therefore we must say that in the divine wisdom are the types of all things, which types we have called ideas—i.e., exemplar forms existing in the divine mind'. Cf. also First Part, ques. 15.

1. As a MS. variant Pope has this line: 'How unideal thoughts now meaning find' (EC, IV, p. 276). Since this refers to the 'works' Dulness shows to her children, it may be an oblique reference again to the divine 'ideas'. Cf. also Pope's 'Index of Matters Contained in this Poem and Notes', where he speaks (*Twick. Ed.*, p. 421) of Dulness's 'Ideas, Productions and Creation ... Her Survey and Contemplation of her Works ... and of her Children'.

2. See I 273 B.

> She saw slow Philips creep like Tate's poor page,
> And all the mighty Mad in Dennis rage. (I 99–106 B)

Then occurs a charged Miltonic phrase which relates the dunces to Dulness as man to God (and Cibber to Dulness as the Son to the Father):

> In each she marks her Image full exprest,
> But chief in Bays's monster-breeding breast.[1]

At another point we see what appears to be a direct travesty by Dulness of God's creation of man:

> All as a partridge plump, full-fed, and fair,
> She form'd this image of well-body'd air;
> With pert flat eyes she window'd well its head;
> A brain of feathers, and a heart of lead;
> And empty words she gave, and sounding strain,
> But senseless, lifeless! idol void and vain!
>
> (II 41–6 B)

Moreover, the dunces, like men, have souls of the same stuff as their Creator—in this case, darkness:

> for then a ray of Reason stole
> Half thro' the solid darkness of his [Settle's] soul;
> (III 225–6 B)

or else they have 'monster-breeding' minds which reflect the un-creating mind of Dulness.[2]

The design to which all these references conform begins to emerge after the episode in which Cibber addresses the children he is about to sacrifice. His words not only give us a historical

---

1. Throughout *Paradise Lost* one finds such phrases referring to the Son of God as this one: 'he all his Father full exprest'. See III 139, VI 270, VII 196, X 66.

2. Pope further conveys the likeness by his hilarious use of the word 'head', which occurs, along with such correlative terms as 'mind' and 'brain', frequently throughout the poem: it is in their minds that the dunces are most like the deity whom one of her sons calls the 'Common Mother of us all'.

Note the mock-religion of this prayer which Cibber addresses to Dulness:

> Great Tamer of all human art!
> First in my care, and ever at my heart . . .
> O! ever gracious to perplex'd mankind,
> Still spread a healing mist before the mind;
> And lest we err by Wit's wild dancing light,
> Secure us kindly in our native night.   (I 163–76 B)

perspective on duncery, but introduce into that history the doctrine of the transmission of original sin:

> O born in sin, and forth in folly brought!
> Works damn'd, or to be damn'd (your father's fault)
> Go, purify'd by flames ascend the sky,
> My better and more christian progeny . . .
> O! pass more innocent, in infant state,
> To the mild Limbo of our Father Tate:
> Or peaceably forgot, at once be blest
> In Shadwell's bosom with eternal Rest!
>
> (I 225–8, 237–40 B)

Shadwell's bosom here corresponds of course to Abraham's, the
traditional source of the idea of Limbo. Because of their 'original
sin' Cibber's 'children', like all who died before the coming of
Christ, must abide in a Limbo, a duncely one.

The really daring nature of Pope's correspondence becomes
even more unmistakable in the next episode. To her chosen race
of dunces Dulness sends a 'Messiah', a duncely inversion of
Christ, able, we may suppose, to 'atone' their literary errors:

> The Goddess then, o'er his anointed head,
> With mystic words, the sacred Opium shed.
> And lo! her bird, (a monster of a fowl,
> Something betwixt a Heideggre and owl,)
> Perch'd on his crown. "All hail! and hail again,
> My son! the promis'd land expects thy reign."
>
> (I 287–92 B)

This fantastic incident derives from Matthew iii:

16 And Jesus, when he was baptized, went up straightway
out of the water: and, lo, the heavens were opened unto him,
and he saw the Spirit of God descending like a dove, and
lighting upon him.
17 And lo a voice from heaven, saying, This is my beloved
Son, in whom I am well pleased.

And to drive home the connection, the poet adds, in the last
edition, 'Lift up your gates, ye Princes, see him come!'[1]

On this level, the complex of allusion centring about Cibber

1. See *Dunciad*, I 301 B. Cf. Psalm xxiv 7: 'Lift up your heads, O ye gates,
and be ye lift up, ye everlasting doors; and the King of glory shall come in.'

begins, perhaps, with the opening line of the poem, where Pope proposes to sing of 'The Mighty Mother, and her Son'. In view of Dulness's relationship to the Almighty Father (in a MS. reading she is called 'Almighty Dulness',[1] and is of course the 'Mighty Mother' throughout), one may see perhaps in the word 'Son' a hint at the Son of God. And when Cibber is called, at the opening of Book II, the 'Antichrist of wit', Pope makes overt the metaphorical and inversive relationship so much of the poem appears to imply. In the opening of Book III the metaphorical connection is made again, this time in a more subtle form:

> But in her Temple's last recess inclos'd,
> On Dulness' lap th' Anointed head repos'd.
> Him close she curtains round with Vapours blue,
> And soft besprinkles with Cimmerian dew.

If we recall that the Messiah is the 'Anointed' and that the Virgin's colours are traditionally blue, it is possible to discover in this portrait a caricatured 'Madonna and Child'.[2] With its extremely covert allusiveness this passage is a good example of the type of theological hide-and-seek Pope forces the reader to participate in.

In the Argument to Book IV the poet states that Dulness will send to her followers 'Priests, Attendants, and Comforters'.[3] Since Christ promised His disciples that He would give them 'another Comforter, that he may abide with you for ever',[4] Warton found Pope's allusion particularly outrageous.[5] The fact remains that throughout the *Dunciad* one encounters the suggestion that Dulness has on earth a kind of 'church' in which the body of her followers are united. Thus the dunces are her 'chosen', they will be led 'To lands, that flow with clenches and with puns',[6] they have had, like the early Christians, to endure persecution for their faith:

1. EC, IV, p. 293, n. 4.
2. The religious direction of the verse is further emphasized by the fact that the 'Temple's last recess' was originally written as 'Temple's holiest holy'. See EC, IV, p. 290, n. 1.
3. Cf. *Twick. Ed.*, p. 338.   4. John, xiv 16-17.
5. Warton objected to quite a few of the allusions as being profane. See his edition of Pope's *Works*, V, p. 120.
6. See I 273 B, I 252 A.

> Here all his suff'ring brotherhood retire,
> And 'scape the martyrdom of jakes and fire.
>
> (I 143–4 B)

The shaggy tapestry Dulness gives to Curll displays 'the fates her confessors endure' (in MS. the line read 'the fates her martyrs militant endure'[1]). The church fathers, such as Eusden, sleep

> among the dull of ancient days;
> Safe, where no Critics damn, no duns molest,
> Where wretched Withers, Ward, and Gildon rest.
>
> (I 294–6 B)

All these suggestions, hints, and allusions by which Pope correlates the history of duncery with the history of Christianity reach their climax in the final book. There the dunces appear to have their own ritual, one which travesties, as we should expect by now, Christian ceremony. In the following lines, for example, certain of Dulness's priests (the epicures) celebrate a Mass, a black one (as befits a satanic cult):

> On some, a Priest succinct in amice white,
> Attends; all flesh is nothing in his sight!
> Beeves, at his touch, at once to jelly turn,
> And the huge Boar is shrunk into an Urn:
> The board with specious miracles he loads,
> Turns Hares to Larks, and Pigeons into Toads.
> Another (for in all what one can shine?)
> Explains the *Seve* and *Verdeur* of the Vine.
> What cannot copious Sacrifice attone?
> Thy Treuffles, Perigord! thy Hams, Bayonne!
> With French Libation, and Italian Strain,
> Wash Bladen white, and expiate Hay's stain.
> Knight lifts the head, for what are crowds undone
> To three essential Partridges in one?   (IV 549–62)

In one passage after another the reader is finally led to interpret the poetic text in an anagogic sense; his attention is constantly turned from a literal or comic level of interpretation, toward a realm of theological significance. In a sense the procedure is one of delicate annexation: to the course of duncely events, and without, for the most part, fracturing the comic sur-

1. EC, IV 202, n. 3.

face, Pope subtly annexes, by a variety of allusive procedures, many of the chief events and circumstances of Christian theology and history.

Throughout Book IV, more and more of the attributes of the Christian God cluster about the shadowy figure of Dulness. Implicit, for one thing, is the suggestion that Dulness is the One to whom the Many, the dunces, return. The dunces are scattered hither and thither, like leaves and locusts, each isolated from his fellows, his attention adhering to a wide assortment of physical *minutiae*—moss, coins, humming-birds—or to himself. Their consideration is given to the part rather than to the whole: the butterfly fancier meddles 'only in [his] sphere', another turns 'Hares to Larks', and still another ('for in all what one can shine') explains the '*Seve* and *Verdeur* of the Vine'. In fierce rivalry these atomistic individuals scorn one another—the fops pushing the pedants out, one specialist quarrelling with another —but in the end they are all assimilated into the being of their Common Mother. At the beginning of the book,

> The young, the old, who feel her inward sway,
> One instinct seizes, and transports away.
> None need a guide, by sure Attraction led,
> And strong impulsive gravity of head:
> None want a place, for all their Centre found,
> Hung to the Goddess, and coher'd around.
>
> (IV 73–8)

At the end, we are told, 'ev'ry finish'd Son returns to thee'; 'Now to thy gentle shadow all are shrunk'; 'Then take them all, oh take them to thy breast'. And at that breast the dunces find the peace of Dulness which passeth understanding: the Almighty Yawn of their goddess in which they too yawn, 'invisible and dim'—their consummated sonship in the Motherhood of God.

Implicit also in the poem is the notion that Dulness is not only God the Mother, but (in one of her aspects) God the un-Holy Spirit. Thus in the final redaction of 1743 the poem opens with a parody of the passage in Genesis which describes the Spirit of God moving over the waters:

> Say how the Goddess bade Britannia sleep,

L

> And pour'd her Spirit o'er the land and deep . . .
> Here pleas'd behold her mighty wings out-spread
> To hatch a new Saturnian age of Lead.
>
> (I 7–8, 27–8 B)

The image is developed further in Book III:

> And see, my son! the hour is on its way,
> That lifts our Goddess to imperial sway;
> This fav'rite Isle, long sever'd from her reign,
> Dove-like, she gathers to her wings again.[1]
>
> (123–6 B)

The earliest version of Book IV (the *New Dunciad* of 1742) closed
with the same theme. In fact, in this intermediary version of the
fourth book, the yawn of Dulness appears to be a humorous
realization of the emanation of the Spirit as it grandly engulfs
creation and returns it to original inertia:

> More had she spoke, but yawn'd—All Nature nods:
> What Mortal can resist the Yawn of Gods?
> Churches and Chapels instantly it reach'd;
> (St. James's first, for leaden Gilbert preach'd)
> Then catch'd the Schools; the Hall scarce kept awake;
> The Convocation gap'd, but could not speak:
> Lost was the Nation's Sense,[2] nor could be found,
> While the long solemn Unison went round:
> Wide, and more wide, it spread o'er all the realm;
> Ev'n Palinurus[3] nodded at the Helm;
> The Vapour mild o'er each Committee crept;
> Unfinish'd Treaties in each Office slept;
> And Chiefless Armies doz'd out the Campaign;
> And Navies yawn'd for Orders on the Main.
>
> O Muse! relate (for you can tell alone,
> Wits have short Memories, and Dunces none)

1. Cf. these lines from *Paradise Lost* (I 19–22):
> Thou from the first
> Was present, and with mighty wings outspread
> Dove-like satst brooding on the vast Abyss
> And mad'st it pregnant.

2. The 'Nation's Sense', or the 'Wisdom of the Nation', were phrases quite often applied in the period to the British Parliament.

3. Referring to Walpole, pilot of the ship of state.

> Relate, who first, who last resign'd to rest?
> Whose Heads she partly, whose compleatly blest?
> What Charms could Faction, what Ambition lull,
> The Venal quiet, and intrance the Dull?
> Till drown'd was Sense, and Shame, and Right, and
>   Wrong—
> O sing, and hush the Nations with thy Song!
> While the Great Mother bids Britannia sleep,
> *And pours her Spirit o'er the Land and Deep.*[1]

At this point the poem gathers itself for the 'crowded thoughts and stately numbers'[2] which culminate in its final climactic theological event—the 'coming' of the one remaining person of the Trinity, the anti-Messiah. Here all the theological implications do break out of their comic wrappings, and assume dominion in the sphere of 'public speech'. In a final sweep of dignity, like a river reaching the sea, the poem at length reveals the powerful undercurrents that have moved within it from the start. The event has been prepared for in Book III, where Cibber, we recall, is given a vision of the future, an apocalyptic revelation of a 'new world . . . with a heav'n its own', corresponding, of course, to the 'new heaven and a new earth' to be created by Christ following the destruction of the old. In the concluding paragraph of the poem the prophecy is fulfilled, and the action merges with the events described in Revelation. Amid the falling stars and flashing meteors of a world she has 'destroyed' we see Dulness, now the transcendent Word, at her second 'coming':

> She Comes! she comes! the sable Throne behold
> Of *Night* Primaeval, and of *Chaos* old!

The 'sable Throne' inverts the 'great white throne' upon which Christ makes *His* Second Advent:

> And I saw a great white throne, and him that sat on it, from whose face the earth and the heaven fled away; and there was found no place for them.[3]

1. Italics mine.
2. This is the way Samuel Johnson describes the poem's close. See 'Life of Pope' in *Lives of the English Poets*, World's Classics Edition, intro. by Arthur Waugh (London, Oxford University Press, 1946), II, p. 338.
3. Revelation, xx 11.

And then, to seal all in darkness and to annihilate creation, there is, in the ending, the 'word', the anti-Logos of Dulness:

> Lo! thy dread Empire, Chaos! is restor'd;
> Light dies before thy uncreating word:
> Thy hand, great Anarch! lets the curtain fall;
> And Universal Darkness buries All.

Since the 'Lord by wisdom hath founded the earth',[1] it is not inappropriately that Pope, in the *Dunciad*, has destroyed it by Dulness, the mighty opposite of Wisdom.[2]

The concluding events of the poem are a procession of images in a phantasmagoric movement by which Pope reveals the powers of duncery at their supreme and final work of bathetic unfulfilment, at their climactic task of negation. For surely the poet in the conclusion of his poem is engaged in a new counterpoise of Longinian sublime and Cibberian profound. In opposition to the sublimity and magnificence attributed by Longinus[3] to the divine command, 'Let there be light', he has involved the dunces in the greatest act of bathos, their deity's command of 'Let there be darkness'.[4]

The inversions of Christian themes and situations in the *Dunciad* cannot be said to function as a formal, precisely determinable 'structure'. But neither, I think, can one dismiss the inversions merely as attempts to achieve rich wit in isolated instances. The inversions are too pervasive a part of the poem's texture to be seen as only scattered and local examples of Pope's ability to manipulate Christian symbols. The very number of the Christian references (and I have cited by no means all of them) necessarily has a wide-spread modifying effect on the events of the poem. Though not forming a structure, the inversions do constitute a net, or a webbing, in which Pope has caught the dunces at their destructive arts. The theological metaphor

1. Proverbs, iii 19.
2. Wisdom and Word were terms early applied interchangeably to the Second Person of the Trinity. If Dulness is the 'uncreating word', then she is almost automatically 'un-wisdom' also.
3. See *On the Sublime*, ix 9.
4. See variant reading, *Twick. Ed.*, p. 192:
> Let there be darkness! (the dread pow'r shall say)
> All shall be darkness, as it ne'er were Day.

(if we can call it that) manages to display the works of duncery in an unholy light, and to make a new kind of darkness visible.

For as Pope employs this principle of inversion in the *Dunciad* it is more than a matter of technique: it is also a realization of the nature of evil, of its negative and destructive qualities. Like Milton, who constructed in Hell a negation of 'the bright clear harmony of Heaven',[1] Pope constructs a world of Dulness which is a negation of the world as known in Christian doctrine. Both poets are attempting, by their inversions, to realize imaginatively the negativism of evil—evil being in Christian thought neither 'an essence nor a nature nor a form' but an absence, a privation, a non-being.[2] And to this end (the shadowing forth of evil) the satanism which enters the poem by means of the Miltonic parody, and Pope's inverted paradigm of a Christian universe, co-operate: the idea of Satan and the idea of Anti-Christ are essentially indistinguishable. Since God, moreover, is the source of all being (and by definition, being, no matter how little, is a good), Dulness, as His inversion, is the source of non-being, of chaos, of the annihilation of the good—is, in a word, evil.

The theological metaphor is the device by which Pope gives imaginative generalization to all the many particular actions of evil committed by the dunces throughout the *Dunciad*. The dunces turn from a higher to a lower good (from God to man, from wisdom to folly) and so commit evil; they misuse, and thus employ destructively, the goods of nature, art, and their own reason—which is the work of evil. For sinning, as St Thomas states, is 'nothing else than a deviation from that rectitude which an act ought to have; whether we speak of sin in nature, art, or morals'.[3] Here, if anywhere, we can realize the propriety of relating bad art to evil, of presenting literary hacks in a satanic context, of calling Cibber the 'Antichrist of wit'. In setting up as poets the dunces, in Pope's view, misuse their own talents and impose upon the 'honest and unpretending' part of mankind.

1. See Maynard Mack's introduction to vol. IV of English Masterpieces, *Milton* (New York, Prentice-Hall, Inc., 1950), p. 16.
2. See Jacques Maritain, *Saint Thomas and the Problem of Evil* (Milwaukee, Marquette University Press, 1942), pp. 1–3.
3. *Summa Theologica*, First Part, ques. 63, art. 1.

In producing bad art under such circumstances the dunces mis-use another good—art itself. And the difference between bad art and good art, and between the forces which produce the two, is finally the difference between creation and uncreation, the creative and the uncreative 'word'.

III

Pope's war with duncery could be called, to sum up, a battle over words—over a destructive use of the 'word', as the poet saw it, by the dunces in the most important areas of human ex-perience: literature, education, politics, religion. There are, in his poem, dunces who, 'impious, preach his Word without a call'; others who teach 'Words alone'; and all are filled with 'empty words . . . and sounding strain'. Wherever Pope turned, such abuses of the 'word' evidently presented themselves to him, abuses which, because of the intimate relation he believed to exist between words and thought, eloquence and wisdom, he could only regard as having injurious consequences for man's well-being. After all, if eloquence *is* a sign of wisdom, then verbal inanity must be a sign of what Pope included in 'dulness'. As Richard Whitlock put it, speaking of certain writers in the seventeenth century (whom he too called 'dunces'), 'behold . . . Ill Language, and Ignorance, as their Matter and Forme coupled'.[1]

In his vision of the Augustan world as a world swamped by hack writings, muddy verse, and party pamphlets, it appeared to the poet of the *Dunciad* that the whole great Western tradition of eloquence, symbol of inner sanity and wisdom, was en-dangered (in a manner to which we have now grown much too used) by incompetent and commercial-minded manipulators of the 'word'. And like others before him, Pope regarded such a situation as symptomatic, thought that a chaotic and malformed rhetoric or poetic reflected an anarchic and malformed charac-ter or mind. Exactly, Seneca had said, 'as each individual man's actions[2] seem to speak, so people's style of speaking often repro-

1. *ZΩOTOMIA, or, Observations on the Present Manners of the English* (London, 1654), p. 160.
2. The facial ugliness attributed to the dunces in the poem is part of the

duces the general character of the time, if the morale of the public has relaxed and has given itself over to effeminacy'. And he continues: 'These words . . . put together so faultily, thrown off so carelessly, and arranged in such marked contrast to the usual practice, declare that the character of their writer was equally . . . unsound, and eccentric'. And finally, Seneca says, 'a lax style, if it be popular, shows that the mind (*which is the source of the word*) has lost its balance'.[1] Pope's contention is precisely that of Seneca: the dunces' writings, their 'words', reflect an inner disorder of the mind, of the 'heads' so often mentioned in the poem.

It is out of such a conception of the 'word' that Pope developed the climactic metaphor of his poem, the comparison of the dunces' 'word' with the Word of God. For the conclusion of the poem and the grandeur with which Pope invests the 'word' of Dulness is not a matter of mere ingenuity on his part: it is a reasonable metaphorical extension of the conception that the human mind engenders its 'word' on the analogy of the Word engendered by the Divine Mind, and this is a conception (whatever many may think of it today) which has had a long and honourable history. In St Augustine's rendering of it, 'our word [meaning, here, an inner word, in the mind, but unexpressed] is so made in some way into an articulate sound of the body, by assuming that articulate sound by which it may be manifested to men's senses, as the Word of God was made flesh, by assuming that flesh in which itself also might be manifested to men's senses. And as our word becomes an articulate sound, yet is not changed into one; so the Word of God became flesh, but far be it from us to say He was changed into flesh'.[2]

---

prevalent tendency to see external characteristics as indicative of inner qualities. In an imitation of the *Dunciad*, *The Censoriad* (London, 1730), the anonymous author says: 'The doctrine of Physiognomy is what hath been always maintained, whence the Latin *Adage*, *Vultus est index animi*.' See note to verse 121.

1. These passages are taken from Epistle cxiv of *Ad Lucilium Epistulae Morales*, trans. by R. M. Gummere, The Loeb Classical Library series (London, William Heinemann; New York, G. P. Putnam's Sons, 1925). For a systematic application of Seneca's principles in Pope's time, see John Brown's *Estimate of the Manners of the Times* (London, 1757).

2. See St Augustine's *On the Trinity*, vol. VII of *The Works of Aurelius*

If we remember that Pope described Dulness as a 'God without a thought', as a 'Divinity without a *Noûs*', then it is evident
that her 'word' will reflect the negative state of her mind, will be
a 'word' of negation, uncreating. Her mind, like that of God,
will produce a 'word' identical with its source. And if the mind
of Dulness is, as Harte said, an embodiment of man's dulness, an
extension of his duncery to a transcendent level, then her 'word'
is also an extension, a sublimated form of all the 'words' that
duncely minds produce. The mind and uncreating word of Dulness are merely Pope's metaphorical dilations of the minds and
uncreating words of the dunces. It is impossible to separate the
war 'over words' which gave the poem its impetus, and the theological metaphor which gives it its profoundest significance: the
poetic ladder which has its foot in dirt does, in metaphoric
fashion, rise to the skies.

The argument has thus come full circle. We are really back at
the starting point of the *Dunciad* and of this essay—in the presence of a very real and lively war between bad writers and a
poet for whom important issues were at stake. Dunces, and
duncely writings, were not, to Pope, matters of little or merely
personal import. Such 'words', such art, inevitably for him referred to states of mind and soul, and to the state of the social
order as a whole. As Pope saw the contemporary situation, such
a 'deluge of authors' (the metaphor is again worth noting) had
covered England that they threatened to 'make one Mighty
Dunciad of the Land'.

Augustine, p. 398. The historical precedents for Pope's analogy between the
dunces' 'word' and the Word of God are so widespread that it would be
remarkable if he had not used them in a poem whose subject is misuse of the
'word'.

Logos has always referred to both reason and speech; the Romans, in fact,
were obliged to translate Logos by the phrase, *ratio et oratio*. It is thus no
accident that Christ is both Wisdom and Word.

INDEX

Addison, Joseph, 24n., 98
Ainsworth, Henry, 140
Akenside, Mark, 145n.
Ancients and Moderns, 12, 45, 104–5
Annius, 90, 124–5, 126
Aquinas, St Thomas, 145n., 155
Archer, Thomas, 92n.
Aristotle, 83n., 105
Arnold, E. V., 118n.
Ascham, Roger, 106, 109n., 113n., 115, 122, 123
Augustine, St, 106, 126n., 145, 157
Ayre, William, 89, 116

Bacon, Francis, 105n., 107n., 114n.
Baillie, David G., vi
Baker, Thomas, 120n.
Baldwin, C. S., 105n., 106n.
Bancks, John, 51n.
Beardsley, M. C., 2n., 3n.
Bentley, Richard, 82, 90, 109, 118, 119, 120, 121, 133
Berecynthia, 26, 27, 51n.
Blackfriars Landing, 33
Blackfriars Wharf, 39
Blackmore, Sir Richard, 9, 11, 36–8, 41, 48n., 95
Boileau, 6
Bolingbroke, Henry St John, Lord Viscount, 99n., 100, 101n., 119
Bouhours, Father Dominique, 14n.
Boynton, Henry W., 63n.
Boys, Richard C., 38n.
Bredvold, Louis I., 10n.
Brett-James, Norman G., 31n., 32n.
Brontë, Emily, 68
Brooks, Cleanth, vi
Brown, John, 13, 108, 157n.

Browne, Sir Thomas, 136–7n.

Caryll, John, 61n.
Casaubon, Meric, 107n.
Ceres, 27
Chancery Lane, 37
Charles II, 10
Charron, Pierre, 107n., 108n., 110n., 120, 129
Chetwood, William Rufus, 53, 75
Christian Socratism, 84
Cibber, Colley, 12, 41, 51, 91n., 100, 132, 135, 136, 138, 147, 148, 149, 155
Cibber, Theophilus, 91
Cicero, 105, 106, 107, 112n., 114, 115
City and Court, 18, 30–9, 88
City Poet, 18, 32, 40
Clarke, John, 112n.
Cleland, William, 85, 86, 95
Courthope, W. J., vi, 5n., 16, 32, 37n., 57, 134n.
Covent Garden, 31
Croker, J. W., 16
Curll, Edmund, 53, 57, 66n., 70, 75, 78, 79, 80, 82, 150

De Bruyne, Edgar, 140n.
Defoe, Daniel, 10
Denham, Sir John, 44, 47
Dennis, John (1657–1734), 16, 29, 55, 70, 72, 74, 75, 80, 85n.
Dennis, John (1825–1911 ?), 6n.
De Quincey, Thomas, 2n., 7
Descartes, 109, 129
Drury Lane, 36
Dryden, John, 7, 117; *Aeneid*, 19, 58; *Albion and Albanius*, 118n.; *Discourse*

159